What People Are Saying About

Paid with a Kiss

I'm always excited to read a new book by Morgan Daimler, and *Paid with a Kiss: Love and Sex in Fairy Belief* was no exception. She delves deep into the folklore behind gender, relations, and sexuality with the Fair Folk in Celtic, Norse, and Anglo-Saxon cultures. Drawing from a rich tapestry of sources including Shakespearean plays, Welsh myths, Scottish ballads, and contemporary literature, Daimler reveals the intriguing world behind the magic. *Paid With a Kiss* was a fantastic vacation into an enchanting world, and is a must-read for both scholars and enthusiasts of fairy belief.

Christy Nicholas, author of *The Druid's Brooch Series*

A brilliant and fascinating look at a little explored aspect of fairylore, I learned something new on every page.

Kelle BanDea, author of *Modron; Meeting the Celtic Mother Goddess*

Rigorously researched while accessible to general readers, this book is a comprehensive guide to the folklore and magic surrounding fairy love and sex throughout history.

Dan Harms, State University of New York at Cortland, co-editor, *The Book of Oberon*

Paid with a Kiss: Love and Sex in Fairy Belief is the most comprehensive, in-depth study of fairy sexuality. Fairy lore, hundreds of years old, combines with anecdotal and first-hand accounts from the 20th and the 21st century respectively to show that fairies never actually left our world, are essentially unchanged, and fairy beliefs significantly still impact us. Morgan tears down the trappings of Victorian and Theosophical alteration of fairy appearance and character, and brings under scrutiny their influence on modern perceptions of fairies. The book traces how fairy lore both reflected and subverted social norms throughout time, thus influencing society's own development particularly in regard to gender roles. Never before fairies' romantic pursuits involving both human and otherworldly partners have gone through such systematic analysis, and their effects on human mores discussed in more unequivocal terms. As a result, *Paid with a Kiss* impacts modern understanding of fairies and of how people relate to them; it holds a mirror for humans to see reflected their own desires, fears, ambitions, potential and flaws, a sight that is equally scary and alluring. *Paid with a Kiss* is a most valuable addition to the existing corpus of scholarly material about fairies and an equally valuable guide for those who seek a personal relationship with these beings.

Daniela Simina, author of *Where Fairies Meet, A Fairy Path*, and *Fairy Herbs for Fairy Magic*

Few things have changed with as much deep-reaching impact as our views on sex and gender in the current era. Perhaps it is for this reason that this topic, when applied to the eternal mystery of the Good Folk, is incredibly crucial, not only to understanding Them, but ourselves in relation to Them. Daimler's work here is lucid, honest, and thorough, giving us an unflinching sense of this interaction from numerous angles.

Lee Morgan, author of *A Deed Without a Name* and *Sounds of Infinity*

Paid with a Kiss is a fascinating journey through the intimate relationships between humans and fairies. Although I was familiar with some of the folktales and stories, we find in this volume a wonderfully researched account of what is to be found on fairy-humans sex and love affairs, and there is more than you think! Fabulous book for those looking to deepen their knowledge about fairy lore and the full spectrum of our connections to the fairy realms. Another must read from Morgan Daimler not to be missed. Beyond informative, a wee gem.

Ness Bosch, author of *Magic Bones Sacred Bones: Stories from the Path of the Bones*

Paid with a Kiss

Love and Sex in Fairy Belief

Paid with a Kiss

Love and Sex in Fairy Belief

Morgan Daimler

MOON
BOOKS

London, UK
Washington, DC, USA

CollectiveInk

First published by Moon Books, 2025
Moon Books is an imprint of Collective Ink Ltd.,
Unit 11, Shepperton House, 89 Shepperton Road, London, N1 3DF
office@collectiveinkbooks.com
www.collectiveinkbooks.com
www.moon-books.net

For distributor details and how to order please visit the 'Ordering' section on our website.

Text copyright: Morgan Daimler 2024

ISBN: 978 1 80341 132 3
978 1 80341 867 4 (ebook)
Library of Congress Control Number: 2024937241

A CIP catalogue record for this book is available from the British Library.

Design: Lapiz Digital Services

UK: Printed and bound by CPI Group (UK) Ltd, Croydon, CR0 4YY
Printed in North America by CPI GPS partners

We operate a distinctive and ethical publishing philosophy in all areas of our business, from our global network of authors to production and worldwide distribution.

Contents

Author's Note   xi
Foreword   xiii
Introduction   xviii

Chapter 1 Gender and Sexuality   1
Chapter 2 Fairies Who Love Humans   8
Chapter 3 Fateful Fairies   16
Chapter 4 Literary Lovers   27
Chapter 5 Early Modern Fairylore   35
Chapter 6 Victorian Fairies   57
Chapter 7 Modern Fairies   63
Chapter 8 Fairies, Humans, and Deviance   71
Chapter 9 Marriage to the Other   75
Chapter 10 Frequently Asked Questions   92

Conclusion   96
Bibliography   100
Endnotes   106
About the Author   111

Dedicated to everyone who has asked me about this
subject across the years.
I hope this provides the answers you are looking for.

With gratitude to Cnuasach Bhéaloideas Éireann for
permission to use excerpts from *The School's Collection*.

Ar mu lennán side, mu rográd, mu adnad i cach ní

Author's Note

This book exists because of a question that was asked at the Ohio State 'Fairies and the Fantastic' conference in 2019, after a keynote lecture by Chris Woodyard. Someone in the audience wanted to know about gender and sexuality among fairies, and I quickly realized that there were no in-depth resources on the subject. I started researching and wrote a short article on the topic then a longer paper (presented at the 2022 Folklore Society annual conference) and then expanded it further into a full-length article. It is one of those subjects that seems like it should be simple but is actually much more nuanced than it appears on the surface. It is also something that many people have expressed an interest in, and I hope that this book can help people find some answers to both how gender and sexuality manifest in fairy folklore and how humans interact with those concepts.

This book is an expansion of my previous work on the subject, including revised and edited material from other articles, and is intended to answer both the original question and also related questions that I am often asked. There is a lot of curiosity around the subject but also a deeply ingrained idea, thanks I believe in large part to Victorian re-writing of fairy beliefs, that fairies are both asexual and also incorporeal, seemingly making the idea of fairy gender and sexuality a non-issue. The truth as always is much more complicated and nuanced than it may first appear.

I personally favour using APA citation in my writing and so throughout this book when a source is being cited you will see the name of the author and date of the book in parenthesis after that. This indicates the book that is being paraphrased in that sentence, both for clarity and to allow readers to further research for themselves if they choose to. I have also included endnotes expanding on points that don't fit neatly into the larger text but are important to touch on.

I hope that this book can serve as a good introduction for readers to the many and long held beliefs around human and fairy intimacy. I may have been overly ambitious in this work, as an exhaustive survey of the entire range of these beliefs is likely impossible, but I believe that what I'm offering here has value nonetheless. This should give curious readers a thorough grounding in the beliefs and concepts that have surrounded the subject for the last thousand years in parts of western Europe.

I think readers should note with this work that some content warnings will apply based on the subject matter. These include discussion of: sex, non-consent or dubious consent, death, kidnapping, and pregnancy.

Foreword

Catherine Heath

*EXCLUSIVE: Forget the tales, fairies are back and
with an attitude*
Jaymi McCann, Daily Express 12/14/2014

Stop me if you've heard this one before.

Young female encounters big bad fae male. Sparks fly. The big bad fae male is well named, because he's troublesome to say the least (some might even say downright problematic). However, there's much more to this otherworldly bad boy than meets the eye. As it turns out, he's something of a "diamond in the rough" ... once you get past a few pesky but significant hard edges. So what if the young female gets bruised (and often worse) along the way! Bruises and trauma are nothing compared with that sweet lifetime access to our boy's Hidden Depths.™ Sure, he may have more red flags than a May Day march, centuries of unresolved trauma, and a thing for spitting out grandiose promises to "set the world on fire" for our girl. But that's not important, because eventually our boy is reformed through the power of love and our luck-plagued couple may even get to live happily ever after...or something.

I should also point out here that our boy probably has pointy ears (important for that fine ear-to-jaw line), and may even have wings as well. (But more about those characteristics in a bit.)

If you are a reader of fantasy romance, then the above outline probably sounds more than a little familiar to you (pun intended). After all, human-fairy pairings have become a mainstay of the genre. However, as you'll discover in this book, fairy-human relationships are far from new. We humans have been telling saucy stories about these pairings for a long, long time.

There is a power in stories and storytelling, an all-pervasive person-shaping power. As a (hopefully) real live human person reading this, you can probably think of at least a handful of stories that have shaped you in some way. We all have stories that empower and stories that bind or hold us back; stories others tell about us and stories we tell about ourselves for good or ill. No story is fixed, though; stories can and do change. And it doesn't really matter whether they change organically over time or are intentionally changed by either ourselves or others. The key point is that they can change. *"Change your story, change your life,"* as the saying goes.

However, what happens when the stories in question involve other-than-human people like fairies and elves? This question is one of the central themes of *Paid with a Kiss*.

Beliefs about fairies have changed a lot over the years. Broadly speaking, fairies have gone from being understood as fearsome, fateful beings associated with potent sexuality and a hefty dose of gender nonconformity, to harmless "nature spirits" with none of their earlier sexuality or subversiveness by the time the Victorians rolled around. Imagine a bunch of child-like figures dressed in flower petals with pointed ears and wings and you won't go far wrong. (Told you I'd get to those.) The absolute opposite of a "glow-up."

In Chapter 6, Morgan writes that, *"change is one of the few constants of fairy belief."* A truism if I ever did hear one. However, if change is a constant in those beliefs, then we need to consider how much of a shaping power those belief-stories have on the fairies themselves (if any). Or in other words: which view of the Good Folk appears to be the truest?

Another constant of fairy beliefs (at least in my opinion) is nuance. On the one hand, a number of accounts recorded in the most recent Fairy Census seem to suggest that newer stories do have some influence over the appearance of fairies or how they present themselves to humans. Some of the descriptions provided by eyewitnesses make comparisons with Tinkerbell, Brian Froud's fairies, and in one example, Gollum from the movie adaptation of *The Lord of the Rings*—all significant departures from what we find in the older sources (Kruse, 2020). However, on the other hand, that same census also recorded accounts that described the beings they encountered in very traditional ways. To quote Dr Simon Young, folklorist and resurrector of seemingly dead fairy censuses in the UK newspaper, Daily Express (McCann, 2014):

People's idea of fairies has changed, but it is odd how many have reported seeing things that resemble centuries-old legends. If you go back 500 or 600 years, fairies make people jump, they see them as fearsome and potentially dangerous beings. This has certainly come back.

So, which stories should we listen to? Which view of the Good Folk appears to be most true? I would argue it's wisest to read or listen to as many stories as possible, but especially the older, scarier stories. There's a lot to be said for learning from other people's mistakes instead of your own.

According to the headline quoted at the beginning of this foreword, the fairies appear to be back—a bold statement considering they've apparently been in a state of perpetual departure since the time of Chaucer. However, according to some corners of the modern Pagan and Witch internet (my own included), that tide of perpetual departure seems to have turned, and instead of going out, is now coming back in. This was the claim made by the author John Beckett in his blog post entitled "The Otherworld is Bleeding Through" (Beckett, 2016). Responses to Beckett's post were numerous, with many noting an increase in otherworldly encounters within their own lives and local communities. However, even within this discourse of return, the topic of human-fairy relationships has largely been neglected and still remains somewhat controversial in some communities. While it's hard to overstate the value of Morgan's work on fairies within this socio-magico-religious context in general, this is especially the case with *Paid with a Kiss*. Hopefully, I don't need to make a terrible pun about them "coming (back) in more ways than one" for you to understand why. (Oops, too late!)

Earlier in this foreword, I asked you to consider which stories or beliefs about fairies appeared to be truer. My recommendation then was to read as much as possible. However, if you believe in fairies and consider them a kind of people—people who might be susceptible to the shaping power of stories—then this question holds an ethical dimension as well. I would argue that when it comes to the fairies, we have a responsibility to take care which stories we choose to feed and tell. This is especially important if we also believe they're in the process of returning. As always, our actions in the present play midwife to the future, so we need to choose well.

The fairies have been in a perpetual state of departure for centuries now. Only time (and perhaps stories) will tell whether that perpetual departure will become a perpetual-return, or whether they'll actually get to arrive this time as well.

And in the meantime, there's always that big bad fae boyfriend – if anyone understands the market value of a kiss, it's him.

Catherine Heath, author of *Elves, Witches, and Gods*

References

Beckett, J. (2016, June 8). The otherworld is bleeding through [Web log post]. Retrieved from https://www.patheos.com/blogs/johnbeckett/2016/06/the-otherworld-is-bleeding-through.html

Kruse, J. T. (2020). *Faery: A guide to the lore, magic & world of the good folk*. Llewellyn Worldwide.

McCann, J. (2014, December 14). EXCLUSIVE: Forget the tales, fairies are back and with an attitude. Daily Express. https://www.express.co.uk/news/uk/546800/Fairy-sightings-on-the-rise-and-this-time-they-re-scary

Introduction

"I have won me a youth," the Elf Queen said,
"The fairest that earth may see;
This night I have won young Elph Irving
My cupbearer to be.
His service lasts but for seven sweet years,
And his wage is a kiss of me."
The Faerie Oak of Corriewater, 1901

Stories of the fairy folk in Celtic cultures, as well as Norse and Anglo-Saxon cognates, for as long as we have them in written material and into modern anecdotal accounts, give a picture of beings that both reflect human sexual morality and distort or invert that reflection. Fairies are beings who can in many ways seem to exist in a world and social structure that mirrors or mimics the humans around them, yet as often as there are examples of fairies tending a farm or working in a mill there are tales of these beings upending the expected social order. This may be most clear when looking at evidence relating to fairies, gender, and sexuality, subjects where the Good Folk may act as either caring spouses or forces of seduction and sexual amorality. Common names for these beings, including elf and fairy, were often used interchangeably with the sexually-natured names of incubi[1] or succubi and many stories of fairies of both genders depict them as sexual and potentially dangerous. In cultures which had strict gender roles for men and women fairies appear both embracing those roles and overturning them, embodying a liminal and fluid state. The template of fairies as sexually and socially deviant allows for fertile ground for humans who wish to take on these same aspects themselves, using a connection to or assumed identity among the fairies to justify their own actions and sidestep more restrictive human ethics. In this way the gender and sexuality of the fairies becomes an outlet for those within human society who break out of contemporary norms. Fairies are the stereotypical 'Other' across literature and folklore and also more literally that which is other than human, yet often analysis of the role of fairies in relation to human norms is only shallowly explored or viewed within a tight context of a particular time and place; by taking a broader and potentially deeper look at the subject a wider pattern can be discerned that establishes fairies as embodying the inversion of human gender roles and sexuality within whatever culture and time they are in.

Etymology and Meaning of Fairy: Defining Terms

The word fairy has been used across English material for centuries but in recent years has gained some controversy as questions arise to the appropriateness of using it as a general term for diverse beings. To begin this work, it's important to establish the way in which the word fairy will be used here, as well as to discuss some of the wider history of the word. For the purposes of this work fairy will be used in a broad sense, in line with its historical context but with an understanding of its modern nuances and problematic application; the text will also include some fairy-adjacent beings who are not strictly speaking fairies but are closely related to the concept. Even among scholars across the 20th and 21st century fairy has not been applied in an equal manner, with some choosing to include all Otherworldly beings in the term while others included only a selection of these beings and still others refined fairy down to a very specific usage applying to a certain type of English spirit.

The word fairy has been in continuous use in English, under various spellings, since the 13th century to indicate a place, the realm of Fairy, as well as beings believed to be from this place and things that have the nature of this place (Williams, 1991). Although it is an explicitly English language term it has and continues to be used as an equivalent term for similar beings in non-English cultures or languages, such as the Irish aos sidhe, and has also been used interchangeably, historically, with terms including elf, goblin, and incubi. How accurate or inaccurate these equivalencies are may be debated but the history of such usage inarguably traces back at least 700 years. As such in this work the term fairy will be used in the wider general sense that it has been used historically, to indicate a being of the world of Fairy, an alternate place connected to and adjoining the human world.

The word's etymology is complex and uncertain, with multiple possibilities, including derivation from nymph and peri, being suggested alongside the popular idea that fairy may be rooted in the Latin 'fata' meaning fate or goddess of fate (Williams, 1991). The fate meaning gives a sense of danger or implicit threat to the fairies, however, the lack of clear textual evidence of the source and history of the word prior to the 12th century French and 13th century English leave its ultimate source in obscurity. In its oldest usage fairy comes into English from the French, fae,[2] and was used as a noun to mean the place of Fairy and an adjective for those things with a fairy-like nature; this could include both beings native to the world of Fairy as well as human witches or enchantresses. The word then, like the beings themselves, reflects both the power to enchant for good or ill as well as the intrinsic idea of breaking human social norms or defying societal expectations.

The wider ideas of fairies being connected to sexuality and human morality, or amorality, may perhaps be initially demonstrated through the shifting use of the word 'fairy' which has across time meant the world of Fairy, beings of that world, and additionally promiscuous human women and homosexual human men. In its oldest usage it was sometimes applied to humans, especially women, who were associated with magical practice or thought to be enchanting in nature, the implication being that the person was a human who reflected something of the magical nature of the world of Fairy. In the 17th century this usage changed from implying a magical nature to implying a promiscuous sexual one, reflecting the idea of fairies as amoral and sexual beings, so that we find the word fairy used as a label for sexually open women (Briggs, 1967). This pejorative use, which existed alongside the more overtly Otherworldly one, would in the late 18th and early 19th century, be used for female prostitutes and in the late 19th century transferred to homosexual men, retaining the implication of amoral and loose sexual behaviour but now also encoded with an implied inappropriate femininity (Young, 2018). Dr. Simon Young, in his article exploring the history of this term as applied to homosexual men 'Gay Fairies: When and Why?' suggests that the term being used for gay men was rooted in the 19th century understanding of fairies as feminine in nature which was also the contemporary idea of what homosexuality was, creating a logical crossover between the terms. This view retains the wider pattern seen since the 1600s of applying the word fairy to humans who are in some way seen as sexually deviant in a way that lines up with the popular perception of fairies at that time.

There has been a movement away from using the term fairy as a catch all descriptor, both in academia and some demographics outside academia. While the term itself has a very long well-established history of general use it is true that it is also often used to translate more precise terms, and in using 'fairy' that way nuance and context is inevitably lost. Using fairy for culturally specific beings like the Aos Sidhe can also be an aspect of colonialism and that must be acknowledged.

Within this text we will be using the term fairy and fairylore [fairy folklore] in a general sense with the understanding that we are discussing a range of Otherworldly spirit beings many of which have their own names. Whenever possible specific names or terms will be used instead of fairy, and we will cover a range of examples of beings who have been labelled as fairies, translated as fairies, or who exist in close proximity to the concept. This wide net approach is being used to provide the clearest possible picture of how these beings in general were understood across western Europe, particularly the Celtic isles, historically and how they are now understood and to provide the best understanding of the wider concepts of sexuality and sex in fairy folklore.

Fairies, Elves, and Incubi

Somewhat muddling an already confusing subject is the way that the words elf and fairy were used interchangeably across hundreds of years. Both terms were also used synonymously with incubi and succubi, blurring the lines between each one, and further complicating it we find each used interchangeably as a noun or adjective.

The connection between elves and incubi goes back hundreds of years in England and Scotland where the terms where often used interchangeably:

Ane elphe, ane elvasche incubus [An elf, an elvish incubus]
R. Sempill, 1583

In the older Anglo-Saxon and early English accounts the term fairies was used synonymously with incubus and succubus, as it was believed that these beings would seduce the unwary. This association between fairies and incubi and elves and incubi was so widely held that Chaucer discusses elves in this way in the 14th century *Wife of Bath's Tale* and Scottish writer Montgomerie describes 'elvish incubi' in his 16th century 'Flyting with Powell'. Moving forward it is important to understand that while we might see these terms and groups of beings as distinct today – sometimes even entirely different classes of spirit being – they were not understood that way for most of history, rather the subjects were treated as fluid and overlapping: one person's elf was another's fairy, was a third person's incubus. While this can be – and often is – confusing for modern audiences it is rooted in a situational understanding of these beings by the people who experienced them which meant that the labels which were applied often reflected both the individual's understanding of spirit beings and also the perceived actions of the spirit. Readers will note various quotes throughout the text which use these terms synonymously, such as the quote beginning Chapter 1, and this must be understood not as a contradiction but a reflection of the way the terms were interpreted and used throughout history.

Three Questions

The bulk of this text is going to be aimed at answering three questions: how have humans understood sex and love in relation to fairies? How do fairies interact intimately with humans? How are these concepts expressed and understood today? To answer these questions, we will examine the wider cultural concepts of gender and sexuality, specific folkloric fairies who are known to interact intimately with humans, literary examples, several key time periods of fairy belief, the connection between fairies, humans, and deviance, and the past and present ideas around fairies in intimate relationships with humans. Every topic has been broken down as much as possible to allow the reader to engage with each easily; the result of this is ten short chapters which each build off the others.

Chapter 1

Gender and Sexuality

This makes it that there are no fairies.
For where an elf was accustomed to walk
There walks now the licensed begging friar himself
In late mornings and in early mornings,
And says his morning prayers and his holy things
As he goes in his assigned district.
Women may go safely up and down.
In every bush or under every tree
There is no other incubus but he,
And he will not do them any harm except dishonour.
Chaucer, Canterbury Tales

To understand gender and sexuality in the context of fairies one must have a basic understanding of gender roles and sexual norms among humans across a similar period. Human sexuality and gender roles have changed across the centuries as the wider cultures they are embedded in have changed, and the way that fairies are understood in relation to these subjects has evolved alongside the human concepts. Sex refers to biological sex and reproduction, and gender to the socially constructed roles expected of people (Lidman, 2013). It is important when considering evidence and folklore from the medieval and early modern period to consider the different social dynamics at play which contrast with modern understandings of gender roles and accepted sexual behaviour. What may now be seen as normative was often previously viewed as deviant, and to understand the ways that fairies move between accepted behaviours and divergent ones it is essential to grasp this history. It is also important to understand the way that different cultures prioritized sex in life; for example, Medieval Europe focused primarily on food and the body after death, seeing sex as less important compared to those two more pressing concerns, while modern Western society in contrast worries less about survival and the afterlife and more about physical pleasure (Karras, 2005). Gender and social norms will naturally vary between regions and periods based on multiple factors, however, generally speaking the concepts across western Europe into the modern period may be summarized as patriarchal, restricting the roles of women to activities based around the home and expecting sexual activity to be restricted to marriage.

In early modern society, socially acceptable, honourable behaviour was woven into the dynamics of the patriarchal worldview according to which both men and women had their duties and certain limits for their doings that they should not transgress. The contemporary "gender politics" was based on patriarchal hierarchy as well as a gender-specific honour code. (Lidman, 2013)

Women were defined by their fertility and sex in ways that reflected their lifelong relationships to men, particularly through marriage (Botelho, 2015). Sexual morality, particularly for women, was strictly regulated because of the intersection of religious and social mores which placed chastity as an essential value for women's honour and placed the responsibility of ensuring proper behaviour on the male relatives of the women (Lidman, 2013). Expectations for men were also restrictive based on gender roles and conceptualization of male gender was multifaceted, including physical appearance, sex, and male identified accoutrements like the beard and sword or dagger, and male social roles included engaging in martial acts and fathering children (Fisher, 2001). As a woman's role was defined by her place in the home and ability to marry and provide children, a man's role was defined by his activities outside that home, his role as a provider, his military skill, and his place as father and head of a household. Or, as Huisman summarizes it in discussing terms for men and women in Anglo-Saxon society:

...in the Old English (and, arguably, in the more general Germanic) usage we have the contrast of a weaving human (female) with a weaponed human (male) (Huisman, 2008).

A person's social reputation and value was predicated on their adherence to these established, accepted social norms.

In contrast the expectations of sexuality and gender roles around fairies often contrast human ones and offer narratives where deviance from the norms and cultural mores are almost expected because of the fairies' own placement outside the usual religious culture. This can be seen across the appearance of fairies in medieval literature where these beings are depicted in blatantly sexual ways and acting outside required gender roles but without apparent moral judgement attached to their behaviours, or the behaviours of humans they interact with (Wade, 2011). These literary fairies are not an exception in the corpus of fairy material, including anecdotal accounts and folklore, but rather are an extension of it and expression of wider views on the fairies' roles while interacting with human societies.

Existing outside the traditional categories the church offered to make sense of the surrounding world, fairies occupied a unique conceptual space that further endorsed the unparalleled freedom with which authors depicted the ambiguous supernatural according to their needs. Far as fairies were from being orthodox, however, it may not be best to describe them as unorthodox either. As recorded and discussed in nonfictional texts...fairies were generally credited as existing in the natural order, but such authorization was allowed precisely because they fit outside any censoring, licensing, or regulating system. (Wade, 2011).

On the surface fairy material may seem to support wider human norms relating to gender and sexuality. In the bulk of recorded fairylore the beings of the Otherworld are described as strongly gendered and sexual, even when they are appearing more effeminate or androgynous. This is supported by an array of fairy appearances across Western cultural folklore and literature. Female fairies are described as stereotypically feminine in appearance, especially in literary works; they are attractive and exemplify contemporary beauty standards. Male fairies may occasionally appear more androgynous or effeminate but are unequivocally male, usually pronouncedly sexual or stereotypically masculine, and when they are seen acting within the gender roles of their time period they are usually depicted as exemplifying the desired masculine qualities. This can sometimes result in the apparent contradictions of a masculine fairy that looks or acts effeminately but is renowned for a typically masculine skill such as blacksmithing, as we see with Völund in the Völundarkviða. In material of all types, fairies are shown as distinctly gendered and often overtly sexual to a point that they were commonly glossed with incubi or succubi. Fairies of medieval literature, often female, take on the role of seductresses and mistresses and only rarely the culturally accepted role of wife. In folklore, ballads, and anecdotes from the 17th century Scottish witchcraft trials, Fairy Queens were known to take human men for lovers, often seemingly on a whim. Male fairies were believed to father children on mortal women, as is referenced in the 14th century 'Wife of Bath's Tale' by Chaucer, and female fairies would sometimes bear children to a human man, as can be seen in the 17th century Scottish witchcraft trial evidence of Andro Man who said that he had fathered multiple children with the Fairy Queen. Prior to the modern period there are no stories in the Celtic, Anglo-Saxon, or Norse milieu showing fairies without an obvious sex, and the link to sexuality is often intrinsic (Wilby, 2005; Hall, 2007). Hall argues that among the Anglo-Saxon the aelfe in the earliest material were inherently transgressional beings who were gendered as male but were notably effeminate in appearance and demeanour, in contrast to the equally supernatural haegtessan who were gendered as female but were notably martial, and hence masculine, in their actions (Hall, 2007). In Anglo-Saxon material, aelfe were so strongly connected to the idea of physical beauty that the term elf-beauty [aelfscyne] is applied to human women of particular attractiveness (Hall, 2007). In the Völundarkiviða Volund, described as the 'king of elves', appears to be a generally effeminate character within the Germanic narrative but is actively sexual, taking a swan-maiden wife, and is renowned for his skill as a blacksmith (Burson, 1983). Volund's wife is also called a Valkyrie, further emphasizing this dynamic, as he stays home while she goes to war. The same point may be argued with the Swan Maidens, a kind of supernatural female being that could appear as a woman or a swan, and who may be equated to other stereotypical fairy wives throughout folklore but are distinctly powerful figures. In these ways fairies in various forms are both familiar and relatable to humans, taking on expected roles such as a blacksmith or a wife, but are also foreign and strange in their defiance of human gender role norms and expectations, acting in ways a human would not.

One example of this is the way in folk belief that Norse alfar and Anglo-Saxon aelfe are initially all male beings, then shift into male and female beings, and later in some areas predominantly female (Hall, 2007). This implies a certain broad fluidity within the beliefs as they relate to the gendering of these beings. Hall also persuasively argues that this fluidity of gender as well as the aelfe's often effeminate depictions reflect a wider understanding of aelfe existing in contrast to the normal daily boundaries created by gender roles (Hall, 2007).

This strong gendering and sexuality offers only part of the wider picture of fairies in the context of human gender roles and sexuality, however. Looking at fairies within specific cultures and time periods the pattern of clear gendering and overt sexuality are readily apparent, however, another divergent pattern can also be found if a wider view is applied. Across the wider breadth of folklore, we also find that while fairies of either gender may appear and act within the expected gender norms for their time and society, they also act against them. There are an abundance of stories in which male fairies appear in domestic roles which would have been seen as female roles within their society, such as stories of Robin Goodfellow who would cause mischief but also assist in the kitchen or farmyard. Further support for the premise is seen in the primacy of Fairy Queens in literature and ballads during periods where kings were usually viewed as the norm and more powerful figures; even when a Fairy King is mentioned in folklore it is usually the Queen who is described as the active force. In the prose tale of Thomas of Erceldoune, the Fairy Queen is out hunting, a typically masculine activity, when she finds Thomas and takes him as her lover; her Fairy King is only obliquely referenced later in the tale, appearing as a shadowy figure to the Queen's powerful and dominant force. In the ballad version of the same story, titled Thomas the Rhymer, she is less overtly masculine but still exists outside human expectations, as Dunnigan describes her: "a vision of physical beauty, associated with active sensuality and the idea of transgression, as sealed by the kiss which is Thomas's teind." (Dunnigan, 2016).

Fairy Queens also broke human boundaries relating to gender by giving knowledge and skill normally associated with women to men, as we see in the testimony of Andro

Man during the witch trials who credited the Fairy Queen for teaching him cunnnigcraft (Purkiss, 2000). Fairies demonstrate a fluidity between accepted human social norms relating to gender and deviance from those same norms. Buccola says that *'Fairy gender identities were, thusly, highly ambiguous...'* and that *'fairies indiscriminately engage in activities socially ascribed to men or women specifically'* (Buccola, 2006). Fairies act outside accepted human gender and social norms, but are not described in ways implying judgment for their behaviour as even those acting maliciously or directly equated to incubi or succubi were not seen as evil but as existing outside human society (Wade, 2011). In other words, fairies were exempt from the usual rules for proper masculine and feminine behaviour because fairies existed outside the bounds of human social structures.

The early modern grimoire material may also offer insight into this aspect of fairies and how they were perceived and understood through a specific cultural context. Although in folk belief and earlier anecdotal accounts there is no indication of gender fluidity among individual fairies the grimoires show a different understanding of these beings with female fairies appearing elsewhere as seemingly male dukes of Hell, albeit understood through a more dominantly Christian paradigm. The inherent sexuality of the fairies is preserved even in these sources, with spells to invoke and bind a fairy to one's will featuring the explicit taking of that fairy as a lover.[3] (Harms, Clark, & Peterson, 2015).

Chapter 2

Fairies Who Love Humans

The woman answered. "He speaks to a beautiful young woman, well-born, who expects neither death nor old age. I love Red Connla. I invite him to Maig Mell [pleasant plain] where ever-living Boadag is king, a king without weeping without woe in his land since he has taken sovereignty. Come with me oh Red Connla .... if you come with me your form will not wither from its youth and beauty until deceitful Doomsday.
Echtra Condla, trans. M. Daimler

Fairies and humans are intrinsically connected across both historic and modern belief; the fair folk are beings who both borrow and steal from humans, who imitate the human world as well as exist beyond it, and who can represent both help or harm. One aspect of this connection that appears across different culture beliefs in these beings is that they can and will abduct humans for various purposes, including abducting women and men to become spouses to fairies and to provide children to the less fertile fairies. Some of these stories clearly have a darker tone, with the human an unwilling participant, but in others both the human and fairy seem to genuinely care for each other.

While we might tend to assume that it would be human women who were the victims or participants in this, that was not exclusively the case. Some of the grimoire material offers ceremonies to invoke a female fairy to be the (male) magician's lover and medieval literature is littered with accounts of human men who had female fairies as lovers, from the Arthurian Launfal with his fairy mistress to Raymond of Poitou's wife, the fairy, or half-fairy, Melusine. Often, as with Keats 'La Belle

Dame sans Merci', this intrinsic sexuality was paired with an equally intrinsic danger or risk[4] to the human.

While modern readers may envision fairies, et al, as incorporeal this is a much newer way to understand these beings. Across history fairies were understood to be physical beings who could tangibly interact with humans, although they were able to control and choose this corporeality. Reverend Robert Kirk, writing in 17th century Scotland described the body of fairies as *"light changable Bodies, (lyke those called Astral,) somewhat of the Nature of a condensed Cloud"* (Kirk & Lang, 1893). This view is a way to explain how beings that can pass through knotholes, pass by invisibly, or fly through the air can also physically interact with the human world even to the point of fathering or conceiving children who then live on in the human world as any other person might.

Throughout this chapter we will briefly look at various specific types of beings translated as fairies or elves or adjacent to those beings in order to better understand the range of these beliefs.

Alfar and Aelfe

Two groups of closely inter-related beings are the Norse alfar and the Anglo-Saxon aelfe, both terms which are usually translated as 'elf' in modern English. The terms elf, alf, aelf, and ylfe all come from the same proto-Germanic root and have widely retained the same meaning, although in modern English elf has acquired a range of specific meanings as well which can muddy the issue. For our purposes here elf/aelf/alf should all be understood to refer to human-appearing supernatural beings somewhat akin to the way Tolkien describes elves but more overtly magical.[5] Because alf and aelf are closely related we will be discussing them together here, but it should be remembered that they represent two different cultural streams of belief.

Aelfe could be associated with illegitimate pregnancies and the idea of aelfe fathering children on mortal women goes back to at least the 13th century in England (Hall, 2007). They were often glossed with incubus and like incubus were believed to delight in seducing human women and to represent the risk of illicit sexual relations. It must also be noted, as briefly touched on in the last chapter, aelfe were originally envisioned as entirely and strictly male beings although male beings who personified female beauty and allure. This seeming contradiction reflected the wider contemporary cultural ideas about Otherworldly spirits inverting human norms, resulting in effeminate, beautiful male aelfe who were stereotypically lustful and virile. This changed by the 12th century when female aelfe start to appear in texts, with the word for them seeming to come into use to translate nymph, but just like their male counterparts they were known for seducing humans (Hall, 2007). These unions could produce children and we see references to them in mythology including Hagen in Thidriks Saga who was the son of a human queen by an alf (Gundarsson, 2007).

Elves – Scottish

Closely related to the aelfe we also find the Scottish elves, beings who often interact with humans. They are found across ballad material, witchcraft trial material, folklore, and even into modern anecdotal accounts as appearing very similar to humans but of a more magical nature and finding a home within Elfland. Accused witch, Andro Man, described them as looking and dressing like humans, playing or dancing whenever they chose to, and as shadows but nonetheless stronger than humans (Hall, 2007). Hall notes that unlike their alfar and aelfe cousins the male elves of Scotland lacked the transgressive associations of femininity or feminine beauty and instead more strongly typified masculine roles. The female elves are called *'fairy lovers'* by rev. Robert Kirk, writing in the 17th century, and likened to succubi, because they will seduce men, but as Kirk claims, are unreliable in their affections (Walsh, 2002). Contrasting this characterization legends around the fairy flag of the McCloud's claim that it was given by the lord's fairy lover, and would bring victory three times if it were raised in battle, seeming to show that she did genuinely care for him and wanted to protect him.

Not all elves were eager to take a human lover though, and we should note that there are accounts of a human's interest in such being rejected. In the ballad of The Elfin Knight, for example, the eponymous elf rejects the human girl's advances, claiming she is too young and then later admitting that he doesn't want to leave his elven wife or children. In general, though we find it's not an uncommon occurrence for elves and humans to have more intimate connections, as reflected in the song traditional Scottish song 'Tha Mi Sgith', sometimes called Buain na Rainich or A Fairy Love Song, which speaks of a female fairy or elf awaiting the arrival of her human lover.

Elves – German

The elves of Germany more closely resemble their Scottish counterparts than the Norse ones, although unlike Scottish elves they weren't renowned for their attractiveness. Simek, in *A Dictionary of Northern Mythology*, suggests that the German elf represents a cultural borrowing from 18th century English folklore, which explains why the stories align more with Scottish and English folklore than Norse. Male elves were associated with typically masculine roles, as the Scottish were, and only rarely took on female roles including fortune telling or blessing children (Grimm, 1888). Female elves are more typically feminine but still operate within an inverse power to human women, controlling their relationships and choosing their lovers in ways that defy cultural norms of the time.

Grimm relates the story of an elven woman who passed through a knothole into a home, lived there as the man's wife and bore him four children, before returning whence she had come, through the knothole (Grimm, 1888). In this story we find an elven woman in the role of wife and as an ancestor to a human family, representing not the wild and dangerous seduction that was associated with these spirits in other cases but a tame domesticity; yet like so many other tales it represents an inversion of human norms as it is the elf wife who chooses to enter the home and relationship and who chooses to leave, demonstrating control over the situation and her husband.

The Aos Sidhe: Looking at the Irish Evidence

The connection between humans and the Good Folk in Ireland goes back well over a thousand years in written material and continues through today. The oldest written account in Irish that we have which includes the aos sidhe, Otherworldly beings commonly translated as fairies in English, is the Echtra Condla which tells the story of a king's son seduced away by a sidhe woman. She appears to him and tells him that she has come from a great fairy mound and because she loves him, she wants him to go back with her, to leave the mortal world behind. In the Echtra Nera, we find the human protagonist, Nera, entering a sidhe [fairy mound] and taking a wife there who bears him a son and eventually leaves with him to go to the human world.

Probably the most well-known account of a human and duine sidhe [fairy person] relationship is that of Oisín and Niamh; Niamh comes from Tír na nÓg to Ireland for the warrior Oisín and brings him back with her to the Otherworld. Oisín is himself half of that world as his mother was a woman of the sidhe who had been (temporarily) rescued by his father Fionn mac Cumhal. Moving out of mythology, at least in part, we find stories in Galway of the Tuatha Dé Danann and Fairy King Finnbheara who had a queen of unsurpassing beauty but was fond of taking human women as lovers. Lady Wilde relates one story of this 'Ethna the Bride' in which Finnbheara steals a bride on her wedding night, only to have her determined husband dig into his sidhe until Finnbheara relents and returns her. Lady Wilde also tells another tale with a very different ending about a man taken to be the groom of a fairy woman; his family hired a fairy doctor to retrieve him but in the end an apparition of the young man seemed to appear which begged them to leave him where he was with his Otherworldly bride (Wilde, 1887).

There are several female members of the Tuatha Dé, now considered Fairy Queens, who are said to be the progenitors of human lineages. This includes Áine, who was said to be the lover of the third earl of Fitzgerald and the mother of the fourth earl. In some accounts either Brian Boru or his son, Donnchadh, was the lover of the Fairy Queen, Aiobheall, who appeared before the battle of Clontarf to warn them and is thought to have a tie to the family line even today.

In conversation once at an event in Clara, Ireland someone told me a story of one of their relatives who, in the 1980s, had disappeared for a week allegedly with the sidhe and returned only to later announce they were pregnant. While the responses to this news were mixed, according to my source, and included both those who assumed that the woman had simply run off for a romantic fling and those who believed her story, it reflects the living layer to this folk belief. Even in the late 20th century suggesting the sidhe were involved raised at least the spectre of possibility.

Gwragedd Annwn: The Welsh Evidence

The Welsh Lake Maidens are a type of being that are renowned for their relationships with humans (Briggs, 1976). In what is perhaps the best-known story a young man sees a Lake Maiden sitting within the water brushing her hair and sets out to woo her. He does this by offering her bread three days in a row; the first day the bread is too hard, the second day it is too soft, but on the third day it is acceptable to her and she agrees to marry him, under the condition that if he strikes her three times she will leave him. This, of course, eventually comes to pass and the Lake Maiden returns to her watery home along with the cattle she brought to the marriage. She leaves behind, however, the children that she had with her human husband who go on to live their lives within the human world.

Beyond these Lake Maiden stories we do find, as with the Irish, stories of mythic or Otherworldly figures, like Rhiannon, who have relationships with humans.

Selkies – Cross-Cultural Seal Folk

"I am a man upon the land,
I am a silkie in the sea.
An when I'm far fae every strand
Ma dwelling t'is in Sule Skerry."
"Alas, alas this woeful fate
This weary fate that's been laid on me,
That a man should come frae the West o' Hoy
Tae the Noraway lands tae hae a bairn by me."
The Great Selkie of Sule Skerrie

Selkies may not properly be considered fairies but are included here as fairy adjacent beings who fit the wider pattern of humanoid Otherworldly beings who have sexual encounters with, and sometimes marry, humans. Selkie folklore can be found in Ireland, Scotland, and Iceland, as well as the Shetland and Orkney isles. The term selkie means 'seal' and these beings are seal-folk who have a seal form in the water but can emerge onto land, remove the sealskin, and appear human.[6] In some folklore this transformation can only occur once a year while in others it seems to be a more flexible concept.

Within selkie folklore we find two strands of belief relating to human relationships. Female selkies are known across the range of stories for being taken, usually unwillingly, as wives to human fisherman. In most versions the fisherman spies on the selkie, or a group of selkies, dancing on a beach and sneaks close to steal her sealskin. Without the sealskin the woman is unable to return to the sea and has little choice but to marry the fisherman, although it often happens that many years later one of her children by that fisherman finds her hidden sealskin and returns it to her. Once she has the sealskin back, she immediately returns to the ocean, sometimes taking her half-human children, other times abandoning them to their father's care. In contrast, male selkies appear in tales as rakish figures who, as in the song 'The Great Selkie of Sule Skerrie', father a child on an unknowing woman only to disappear afterwards. Selkie men could be invoked by those who wanted such a tryst if the human woman cried seven tears into the sea and wished for a selkie lover (Briggs, 1976).

This is an overview of the beliefs related to specific types of beings who are often labelled as or associated with fairies, from Iceland to England, Scotland to Germany, Ireland to Wales. While the details and specific beliefs can vary the idea that these beings can have an active desire to engage romantically and sexually with humans is clear across all the stories. These are beings who can be lovers or spouses, who produce children with their human partner, but who operate under a very different social structure and apparently different morals.

Chapter 3

Fateful Fairies

I met the Love-Talker one eve in the glen,
He was handsomer than any of our handsome young men,
His eyes were blacker than the sloe, his voice sweeter far
Than the crooning of old Kevin's pipes beyond in Coolnagar.
I was bound for the milking with a heart fair and free–
My grief! my grief! that bitter hour drained the life from me;
I thought him human lover, though his lips on mine were cold,
And the breath of death blew keen on me within his hold.
(Carbery, 1902)

It would be impossible to discuss the subject of fairies and sexuality without also noting the way that these beings often depict sexuality at its most dangerous. This is particularly, although not exclusively, true of female fairies in relation to male humans; as Dunnigan concisely explains it:

The supernatural feminine, as here portrayed in these late medieval, early modern, and traditional incarnations of the fairy world, positions men as both the victims and beneficiaries of its powers (Dunnigan, 2016).

This emphasizes the way which the female fairy overthrows the human societal norms by positioning fairy women as powerful, potentially harmful figures in contrast to their human counterparts who are depicted as ideally demure and supporting the home and by extension the social order. Male fairies may also be portrayed as dangerous, as we find in the anecdotal accounts from Scotland's witch trails where female witches would mention having a male fairy, sometimes described as an assumed-dead male relative now among the fairies, who would act as a guide to them but who could also be threatening or cause them harm when they balked at doing the fairies' will. Speaking very generally, however, male fairies are not as often shown to be physically dangerous in this same way as female fairies may be across literature and folklore but instead may take on domestic and supportive roles that would usually be expected of human women, thus giving us a true inversion of the gender roles from humans to fairies.

The physical danger presented by sexual encounters with fairies is not always seemingly intentional but sometimes appears as an accidental consequence of intimacy with the fairies as Purkiss describes when recounting a tryst between a Fairy Queen and mortal man:

> *Once, [the queen] had had intercourse with him three times in a row, and had then 'sucked up her breath' at the moment of climax, so that she had drawn 'the very substance of the marrow' out of his bones. She had almost killed him.* (Purkiss, 2000).

In that encounter it didn't seem to be a characteristic of the fairy being described to cause death or harm during sex but rather the harm resulted because of the unrestrained passion of the fairy in that moment. Along the same lines in 20th century anecdotal accounts of Scottish diasporic fairies in Newfoundland there are descriptions of young women having encounters with fairies while picking berries that seem overtly or subtly sexual and often contain mentions of physical harm, violence, or social consequences (Narvaez, 2000). Narvaez connects this dangerous sexuality to both an expression of human anxiety towards sexual maturity as expressed in folklore as well as an aspect of the wider nature of fairies which equates the fairies' place outside of human time to their position outside human morality.

Since temporal continuity and a sense of absolute morality are one and the same, threats to moral order were ruptures in time, and this danger was an essential element in the "threatening figure" role of fairies... (Narvaez, 1991).

Across the various folklore we find a range of fairies who have sexual encounters with humans, sometimes with negative consequences for the human, sometimes with better results. But within this wider subject we find some types of fairies who have or who have gained a reputation for being both sexual and predatory towards humans in a way that puts them into their own category, apart from the usual run of fairy relationships. These are beings who use seduction as a weapon, manipulating their victims to make them vulnerable. In most cases though when these stories are dug into, we find that even these dangerous beings seem to have either been created during the Victorian era or profoundly rewritten during that period, perhaps to suit mores and tropes of the authors recording them. While we can certainly find examples of fairies who were dangerous to their human lover or caused them harm, intentionally or otherwise, the idea of types of entirely deadly seductive fairies seems to be largely a product of the 19th century, perhaps drawing from the 1819 poetic example of 'La Belle Dame sans Merci'. With that in mind we will explore the fairies who now have a reputation for offering love with one hand and death with the other.

Leannán sidhe

The Leannán sidhe are one of the more fascinating beings across folklore. The concept, as we shall see, has deep roots in Irish folklore going back to the 10th century but was massively rewritten in the 19th century by WB Yeats – so massively that his depiction came to be seen as the standard and then the entire concept subsequently was attacked as his creation. However, despite claims to the contrary, Yeats did not invent the Leannán sidhe whole cloth nor is he the origin of the term. In point of fact references can be found to Leannán sidhe dating back to the 10th century and even appear in 17th century Irish Bibles as the Irish term favoured to translate 'familiar spirit'. So, who and what then are the Leannán sidhe and how did Yeats change them?

The term Leannán sidhe – lennan side in older Irish – is straightforward, it means 'fairy[7] lover' or 'fairy sweetheart' referring to any Otherworldly being of any gender who took a human lover. We find the term Leannán sidhe used in this oldest and most literal sense in 10th century stories of the dal gCais family, notably Brian Boru and his sons. The stories say that Aoibheall was a Leannán sidhe, a fairy lover, to one of the men of the family and appeared in an attempt to protect them before the Battle of Clontarf by warning them of what was to come and trying to convince them to refuse the fight (Ossianic Society, 1854). It is worth noting that Aoibheall more generally may be seen as a sovereignty goddess, a factor that likely tied into the stories of her as a lover of the king or his heir. In the 12th century the term is used for a woman of the sidhe that Finn mac Cumhal takes as a lover, mentioned in the Acallamh na Senorach.

By the 17th century the term was being used to translate 'familiar spirit' in the Irish language versions of the Bible, notably Isaiah 3 and Samual 8 of Bedell's 1642 'Leabhuir na Seintiomna'. Keating's 1634 'Foras feasa ar Eirinn' includes this: *"...the aerial demons [fairies] who were their leannan sidhe during the pagan age [gave them this knowledge]"* and O'Donovan in 1856 uses the term in a similar way in a retelling of the conception of Lugh, blurring the lines between familiar spirit and fairy lover:

Mac Kineely, however, had a Leanan-sidhe, or familiar sprite, called Birog of the Mountian, who undertook to put him in the way of bringing about the destruction of Balor.

The 1854 issue of the Transactions of the Ossianic Society discuss the Leannán sidhe in some depth, describing them as a spirit which will appear in the opposite gender of the human they favour and who offer supernatural aid, but also discusses them appearing as male figures to help warriors in battle. They refer to them as a type of familiar spirit and also as the "Irish Genius" and the text discusses them as both warriors and as inspirers of poets – of any gender – who they eventually steal away to the Otherworld. There is also an account of an exorcism of a male Leannán sidhe from a woman named Shiela Tavish, who he had apparently been tormenting, in which the Leannán sidhe is also called an incubus.[8]

We can also find non-mythic or folkloric uses of the term as well, such as in the case of an Irish bean feasa [wise woman] named Eibhlín ní Ghuinníola in the 19th century who was said to have a Leannán sidhe who taught her herbal medicine and cures (Ó Crualaoich, 2003). This male spirit was physically seen by several people with Eibhlín ní Ghuinníola and was referred to as her Leannán sidhe.

Yeats, however, envisioned the Leannán sidhe as the poet's dark muse, a being who inspired but simultaneously shortened the life of the artist:

The Leanhaun Shee (fairy mistress), seeks the love of mortals. If they refuse, she must be their slave; if they consent, they are hers, and can only escape by finding another to take their place. The fairy lives on their life, and they waste away. Death is no escape from her. She is the Gaelic muse, for she gives inspiration to those she persecutes. The Gaelic poets die young, for she is restless, and will not let them remain long on earth– this malignant phantom. (Yeats, 1888).

This is obviously in stark contrast to the other folklore related here, but may be more in line with related Manx folklore. In

Manx stories the Lhiannon Shee was seen as a vampiric being who haunt streams and wells and would find a solitary man, who she would then seduce and slowly kill (Briggs, 1976). Despite the bulk of material showing this being as no more or less dangerous than any other fairy, the view of the Leannán sidhe as strictly female, alluring, and deadly to her lovers has come to dominate the concept.

Gean-cánach

The Gean-cánach, like the Leannán sidhe, is a being who suffered from being largely rewritten by Yeats. In older sources and in modern folklore across the Gaeltacht [Irish speaking areas of Ireland] the Gean-cánach is effectively synonymous with the Leprechaun as he is known in modern folklore – a type of solitary Otherworldly shoemaker known for trickery. In fact, if one looks the term up in Ó Dónaill's 1977 *Fóclair Gaeilge-Béarla* the definition given for it is *"fairy cobbler"*. The stories we find are exactly what one would expect of a Leprechaun story, as seen in this early 20th century example:

Near the home of the above – named Joseph Reilly lived long ago a farmer named John Reilly, who was fond of gold. On his farm there was a fort. One evening at sunset, as he was taking home a horse that was grazing near the fort, he saw a little man about a foot and a half in height. He wore a red jacket and cap and green breeches. Reilly thought this was his chance of obtaining a large sum of money. He rushed towards the Geancanach, and after a short chase caught him. He brought him home, put him in a box and locked it, intending to hold him until he obtained the information of hidden gold. At last the fairy told him he would show him where he would find a crock of gold on condition he got liberated. Reilly said "That's a bargain". The fairy told Reilly to procure a red string and to go with him to a certain field. They walked along until they reached the field.

It happened to be covered over with "bohalans".[9] Pointing to one of them the Geancanagh said. "This is the spot where you will find the gold. Tie your string on this boholan. It will be your mark. Dig five feet under it and there you will find a large flag covering a crock of gold. Now you must liberate me". Reilly did so and went home for his laize and shovel, to dig for his treasure. On arriving back he went straight to the bohalan with the red string on it but to his surprise he found that every bohalan in the field had a red string attached to it, and no treasure was to be found. (Dúchas, 2024).

The Gean-cánach under the anglicized name 'ganconer' appeared in two stories in a literary magazine in 1826; in both stories they are depicted much in line with general Irish fairies with the first tale focusing on a human man helping a lonely 'ganconer' attempt to find a new wife and the second revolving on a stolen cow (Dublin and London Literary Magazine, 1826). This use of the term as a general equivalent for fairies in toto is found elsewhere as well during that time period, eventually becoming a closer equivalency with Leprechauns specifically.

This is straightforward enough but for some reason Yeats chose to take this same being and make them into the male version of his exclusively female Leannán sidhe. He explains the name Gean-cánach as 'love talker' and his Gean-cánach are seductive male fairies who linger in wild places smoking a clay pipe called a dudeen:

Another diminutive being of the same tribe as the Lepracaun, but, unlike him, he personated love and idleness, and always appeared with a dudeen in his jaw in lonesome valleys, and it was his custom to make love to shepherdesses and milkmaids. It was considered very unlucky to meet him, and whoever was known to have ruined his fortune by devotion to the fair sex was said to have met a gean-cánach. (Yeats, 1888)

This was expanded on in 1902 by Ethna Carbery in her poem 'The Love Talker' where she described the Gean-cánach as a seductive spirit and explains that women who encounter him waste away to a slow death (Carbery, 1902). Her description fleshed out the character as created by Yeats and establishes the understanding of these beings that is found across belief in many places today. The Gean-cánach becomes a seductive and deadly fairy, a being who lures solitary women into carnal relations after which they slowly pine away and die.

Baobhan sìth

A Scottish example of this type of seductive and dangerous fairy being can be found in the Baobhan sìth. The name translates from Gaidhlig roughly to 'dangerous fairy woman' which aptly describes her appearance in stories. Mackenzie describes her this way:

> *A particularly fierce female demon called Baobhan sith might appear as a hoodie crow or raven, or as a beautiful girl of human nature clad in a long, trailing, green dress which concealed the deer hoofs she had instead of feet. Like a vampire, she drank the blood of her human victims.* (Mackenzie, 1935)

There are only a handful of stories about these beings, largely from the 19th century, and they are all strikingly similar. I will paraphrase them here: A group of young men are out hunting when it grows dark so they seek shelter in a small hut or hunting bothy. In the process they are joined by a group of lovely women, in an equal number to the men, who either ask for entertainment or offer it and the group goes inside where one of the men begins singing or playing an instrument while the others dance with the women; as the man entertains them one of the women stays near him clearly waiting to get his attention. At some point the man who isn't dancing becomes aware that something is wrong, often noticing that his friends have fallen oddly silent and sometimes noticing blood. He realizes that the other men are all dead and, in a panic, flees with the women pursuing him, especially the one who had lingered near him as he entertained the others. Eventually he takes refuge among the horses where the women are warded off by the iron of the horses' shoes. The next day when the sun rises the survivor flees to the nearest town and returns with a search party who find his friends all dead in the bothy. In some versions they have been drained of blood, in others their hearts have been torn out.

The Baobhan Sìth then are beings who are seductive and dangerous by nature, seeking out young men who can be lured by their charms and then killing them.

Kelpies

Oh brown haired Morag
Come back to thy little son
And thou shalt get
A speckled salmon from the loch
The night is wet and showery
For my son in the shelter of a knoll...
Cumha an Eich-Uisge

Kelpies are fascinating beings, who may only loosely be labelled as fairies but are being included here for the same reason selkies were included in Chapter 2, as fairy adjacent beings who have a connection to humans via marriage and sexual relationships. In point of fact, they might have been placed into Chapter 2 except that their amorous relations to humans take second place behind their tendency to treat humans as a food source.

Kelpies are a type of Each Uisge or water-horse, in Scottish folklore who appears as a fine black or white horse and lures people into riding it, only to plunge with them into a lake or river, then drown and eat them. Unlike some other water-horses, however, Kelpies can also shape shift into a human form, in which they seduce the unwary. In many versions of that story the kelpie trysts with a human lover then falls asleep with their head in the human's lap, at which time the human notes the water plants or sand intwined in the kelpie's hair and realizes their true nature. In some versions of the story the human then carefully sneaks away, while in others the person is forced to cut away their cloak or hair to escape without waking the kelpie.

There are, however, another strand of stories in which a male kelpie falls in love with a human woman, which can end one of two ways. In some cases, it was said the human woman would be stolen away and kept under the lake in the kelpie's home, usually for a year and a day before she makes good her escape, leaving him with their child (Kennedy-Fraser & MacCloud, 1909). In other versions the woman isn't kept under the lake but rather the kelpie pretends to be human and the two marry with the woman none the wiser about her new husband's equine-fairy nature. In these versions of the tale the woman eventually bears a son and while he is still a baby, she finally realizes what her husband actually is and flees, leaving the heartbroken kelpie to raise their child alone (Bassin, 1977). This story is attached to two lullabies from the Isle of Skye, 'Water Kelpie's Lullaby' and 'Cumha an Eich-Uisge'. These are fascinating inversions of the usual gender roles around mothering, where the male kelpie is left to sing his child to sleep as a mother would be expected to (Kennedy-Fraser & MacCloud, 1909). The songs are also as much lament as lullaby, with the kelpie both singing to soothe his child and also imploring the human mother to return to them.

In one atypical version of the story the kelpie is tamed with a silver bridle and is given a choice to wear it for a year and become human – and earn the right to marry his human lover – or to return to his own world; he chooses to become human (McNeil, 2001). This is an interesting reversal of the usual pattern of these stories.

Chapter 4

Literary Lovers

He fond yn the pavyloun
The kynges doughter of Olyroun,
Dame Tryamour that hyghte;
Her fadyr was Kyng of Fayrye,
Of Occient, fer and nyghe,
A man of mochell myghte.
In the pavyloun he fond a bed of prys
Yheled wyth purpur bys,
That semyle was of syghte.
Therinne lay that lady gent
That after Syr Launfal hedde ysent,
That lefsom lemede bryght.[10]
Sir Launfal, The Middle English Breton Lays, mid-14th century

Many famous fairy lovers can be found in literary sources, often working their way from there into popular belief, but these tales tend to also reflect wider beliefs about fairies of their time. While they must be understood in the context of fiction, their impact is worth noting and particularly the way that these stories have shaped later understandings of fairies, especially fairy woman, as lovers to and of humans. The literary fairy stories have also gone a long way to flesh out our image of the world of Fairy and its inhabitants as they offered more details and more dramatic descriptions than most previous mythic appearances of these beings, particularly in the Irish. Where Connla's mysterious fairy woman is not physically described nor is her home in the Echtra Condla, the fairy women of later continental and English literature are overflowing with detail.

The fairies of Literary Romance are themselves not very romantic by modern standards. These are not beings who gently woo their human partner, nor are they beings who engage with a modern concept of romantic love. The fairies of literary romance are highly contractual creatures whose relationship with their human lover rests on promises and reciprocal obligations; the fairy offers herself as a lover, sometimes additionally offering worldly wealth, and in return the human promises to follow a restriction set on them by their lover. This contractual approach to the relationship is based in a need to equalize the partners, to bring the powerful fairy to earth and to raise the human into a position where he can offer something of equal value (Spyra, 2020). In many stories the human fails and almost always loses his fairy lover, such as we see with Melusine and with Sir Launfal, although his fairy does keep him in the end.

In this chapter we will explore a selection of literary appearances of fairies engaging in relationships with humans, to demonstrate the variety of the texts and also show some of the common themes.

Melusine

The story of Melusine has been told in various texts across cultures, beginning in the 1380's in France with Joan d'Arras', 'The Romans of Partenay or of Lusignen: Otherwise known as the Tale of Melusine' which would be translated into German in the 1450's and then into English by the 1500s. Katherine Briggs classifies Melusine's story as a French version of the fairy-bride trope, in which a mortal man marries a fairy woman but must adhere to specific taboos in order to keep her (Briggs, 1976). In the tale the fairy Pressyne marries a mortal widower, under the condition that he not visit her when she gives birth; she bears him triplet daughters and, inevitably, he breaks the agreement and comes to see her at which point she vanishes with the newborns. One of these daughters is Melusine, who, with her two sisters, would later set out to avenge themselves on their father, an act which their mother punished by turning Melusine into a snake below the waist. The curse was intermittent and could be broken if Melusine found a husband who would agree to never see her on a Saturday. She wandered through France, eventually becoming the queen of the fairies in the forest of Colombiers, until finding a man who married her under the agreement to not see her that one day of the week. All was well at first, but each of their children was born with a deformity and her husband eventually grew suspicious that she was being unfaithful and broke his word by spying on her on a Saturday. He initially said nothing of this, but when one of their son's killed another son, he pushed Melusine away, calling her a serpent, at which time the curse returned and she fled through the air.

Although technically half fairy and half human, Melusine is regarded as fully a fairy, following a pattern of children born to these relationships being considered either fully one or the other type of being. Robin Goodfellow is another example of this, a child born of a human mother and fairy father who nonetheless comes to be understood as a fully fairy being.

Melusine's story reflects many patterns found across both literary and folkloric fairies, with the romance between the human and fairy characters being complicated – and eventually destroyed – by a prohibition that they must live with, and with the human partner largely unaware of the nature of his spouse. Wimberly in *Folklore in the English and Scottish Ballads* also notes that there is a recurrent theme connecting snakes to fairy lovers, something that is seen rather blatantly in Melusine's story.

Sir Launfal

The Arthurian tale of Sir Launfal dates to the mid-14th century and centres on a knight, Sir Launfal, who has a fairy lover.

As the tale opens we find the eponymous Launfal as King Arthur's steward; he is driven away by a mutual animosity with Arthur's new queen, Guinevere, and falls into hard times in a small town. Eventually he goes into the local forest where he finds – or is found by – Triamor, the daughter of the Fairy King, who takes him as her lover, gives him lavish gifts, but extracts a promise that he will not speak of her to anyone, or else she will leave him. Things take a turn when Launfal, once again successful thanks to Triamor, returns to Arthur's court where Guinevere attempts to seduce him. When he rejects her, she accuses him of disliking woman and he foolishly proclaims that his lover's maid is more beautiful than Arthur's Queen, enraging Guinevere who then tells Arthur that Launfal had propositioned her and lied about his mistress when Guinevere rejected him. Because he broke his agreement with Triamor his wealth and success vanish and Arthur wishes to see him hanged, but a jury of his fellow knights declare that if Launfal's mistress can be proven real he will be acquitted. Launfal, however, admits he cannot summon his lover, so he prepares for his fate. Just before he would be executed Triamor appears and saves him, after which the two ride off to her Fairy realm together.

Launfal's tale again reflects the inherent power that the fairy lover has in the relationship, a distinct difference from the social dynamics within contemporary human cultures where it would be the man who controlled things. This reversal is shown in the way that Triamor grants and withdraws her favour, and with it Launfal's luck, as well as the way that it is she who chooses him as her lover. This tale is different in a key aspect though, because unlike other stories where the scorned fairy lover never returns or is seen again by their human partner, Launfal's Triamor shows up in the 11th hour to save his life and more than that takes him back with her into her own world.

Thomas of Erceldoune

A historic figure of the 13th century in Scotland, Thomas of Erceldoune, would be immortalized in prose and later ballad, as well as folklore. In the 15th and 16th century versions of his story it was said that he was laying under a tree on a hillside when he saw the Fairy Queen hunting and drew her attention. He demanded she become his lover, despite her warnings that if they became lovers, she would lose all her beauty; the two had sex seven times after which the queen's appearance changed from young to old and withered. Despite this, Thomas remained with her, riding with her on her horse back to the world of Fairy. Once back in her own world the Queen's beauty returned, but she warned Thomas not to speak to anyone else but her while he remained there, as her husband was very jealous. He stayed with her for three days, after which she sent him back to protect him from both her husband and the fairies' tithe to Hell. When he leaves, he is given the gift of prophecy, a payment for his service to the Fairy Queen.

Thomas is particularly interesting to note among these examples because he is based on a historic figure and because, unlike most others, he is taken out of the human world and into Fairy to be with his Otherworldly lover. He also shows more autonomy than many of the male figures in these examples, as it is he who wants to have sex with the queen without her making any attempt to seduce him, and indeed he who insists on it when she initially refuses him. Her transformation from beautiful to ugly to beautiful again is perhaps an interesting echo of older stories about the goddess of sovereignty changing appearance to test a would-be king's worthiness, although here it is used to test her lover's resolve and dedication.

Shakespeare

One of the key plot points in Shakespeare's 1596 play, *A Midsummer Night's Dream*, is the relationship between the Fairy

Queen, Titania and the human, Nick Bottom. Although it is comedic in nature and based on Titania being struck with a love potion, it nonetheless displays the concept of a fairy as the lover of a human as it was embedded in the folklore and literature. Nick Bottom with his cursed donkey's head epitomizes all that is earthly and bestial in humans while Titania is the epitome of the refined Fairy Queen, bestowing blessing and love on her erstwhile human lover. As exaggerated as this situation is, intended to be played for laughs as the besotted Fairy Queen decks his long ears with flowers and orders her attendants to dote on Bottom while he is requesting things like hay and a handful of dried peas, it nonetheless reflects the pattern observed across many other stories, only with Puck's love potion to explain the usually inexplicable draw between ephemeral fairy and all too terrestrial human.

Less overtly we find Mab in the 1597 play *Romeo and Juliet* as a character who doesn't explicitly take a human lover but is very much involved with them. Mercutio declares that it is Mab who gives lovers dreams of love and ladies dreams of kisses and who:

> *...when maids lie on their backs,*
> *That presses them and learns them first to bear,*
> *Making them women of good carriage.* (Act 1, scene 4)

She is then a spirit who brings desire for love and intimacy through the dreams of humans, who encourages them and even perhaps directly assists.

La Belle Dame sans Merci

I would be remiss not to include the 19th century poem 'La Belle Dame sans Merci' here, as it was written at the end of the era of romantic fairy lovers, a transitional period between the power and seduction of the romances of the previous centuries and the infantilization and disempowering of the ensuing Victorian era. Within this uncertain middle ground, we find a fairy described as both overtly seductive and overtly deadly. This 1819 poem by John Keats depicts a fairy woman who enchants a knight; the name of the poem, 'La Belle Dame sans Merci', means the beautiful woman without mercy.

After encountering a beautiful fairy woman, a knight is led to her bower where it is implied they have a tryst before he falls asleep. He dreams of an array of warriors, princes, and kings who all warn him that he is under the enchantment of the Belle Dame sans Merci. He wakes up from this dream alone on a hillside and begins to pine away, doomed to die and join the apparitions he saw in his dream.

> I met a lady in the meads,
>   Full beautiful — a faery's child,
> Her hair was long, her foot was light,
>   And her eyes were wild.
> I made a garland for her head,
>   And bracelets too, and fragrant zone;
> She looked at me as she did love,
>   And made sweet moan....
> She took me to her Elfin grot,
>   And there she wept and sighed full sore,
> And there I shut her wild wild eyes
>   With kisses four.
> And there she lullèd me asleep,
>   And there I dreamed — Ah! woe betide! —
> The latest dream I ever dreamt
>   On the cold hill side.
> La Belle Dame sans Merci

This poem plays with the idea of fairy romance as dangerous, a moment of joy which costs the human their life as they are consumed by their immortal lover. The fairy woman is enchanting and irresistible but also inevitably deadly, her mortal lover consigned to the ranks of all those previous humans who have given her their love and faded from life afterwards.

Chapter 5

Early Modern Fairylore

...there was a King and Queene of Phairie, of such a jolly court and train as they had, how they had a teynd, and a dutie, as it were, of all goods; how they naturallie rode and went, eate and drank, and did all other actiones like natural men and women.
James VI, *Daemonologie*, 1597

Early modern fairy belief around the topic of humans and fairies is complex, more so than the examples we can find among literary fairies. These are 17th and 18th century examples of living belief which reflect the allure and danger of a human connecting intimately with fairies, showing both people who had seemingly fulfilling relationships with these beings as well as those who suffered for it. The early modern period also shows the immediacy of these beliefs for many people, for whom fairies were not abstract concepts or literary characters but real and tangible beings with an ability to influence a human's life. One pattern which persists though is that of the human as the weaker or powerless partner and the fairy or fairies as the stronger and more powerful or knowledgeable partner(s). Even in the story of Ann Jefferies, below, we see the fairy as the one who initiated the experience and the sexual encounter and the fairies in a wider sense as Ann's teachers and providers, caring for her even when the humans around her do not. Similarly in the 17th century Scottish witchcraft trial accounts we find stories of amorous encounters with fairies wherein the human has little to no control, even to the point of coercion being used against them. The ballad material, which will also be examined here, has a more romantic tone to it but continues this established pattern to varying degrees. In early modern folklore the fairy is the instigator and arbiter of the relationship.

Ann Jefferies

An example of association with fairies interacting in a sexual way with a human can be found in 17th century Cornwall with Ann Jefferies. She was, by her own account, accosted by fairies and fell into an illness marked by what were described as 'fits', after which she claimed to have an ongoing relationship with the fairies and the ability to heal with the laying on of hands and with salves she said were given her by the fairies. Ann was an atypical person before her first fairy encounter, described as *"unusually bold"* and *"refusing to conform to social standards"* (Hunt, 1903; Buccola, 2006). Although she was a servant to the Pitt family, she was given greater freedom and cared for when she was ill as if she were a family member, according to Moses Pitt, the son of the family who employed her. Her story of the first time she met the fairies was explicitly sexual but was received by all accounts without any judgment by those around her and there is no evidence that she was treated differently or badly because of the events she recounted:

> *This [fairy] looked so sweetly on Anne that she was charmed beyond measure, and she put down her hand as if shake hands with her little friend, when he jumped into her palm and she lifted him into her lap. He then, without any more ado clambered upon her bosom and neck, and began kissing her. Anne never felt so charmed in her life as while this one little gentleman was playing with her; but presently he called his companions and they all clambered up by her dress as best they could, and kissed her neck, her lips, and her eyes.* (Hunt, 1903)

Her connection to the fairies eventually led to her arrest, in part because of rumours that she didn't eat human food but was fed by the fairies; the magistrate ordered her held without food which was done but Ann showed no ill health from it and continued to claim that the fairies provided her with bread (Briggs, 1976). While the fairies did lead her into legal trouble her connection to them allowed Ann Jefferies a greater freedom than would have been typical for a person of her status in the time and place that she lived, and her fairy-given healing created a good reputation for her, if not wealth, as she refused to take any money for what she did.

The Witchcraft Trial Accounts

Individuals, particularly witches and cunningfolk, who lived outside or on the margins of human society were often connected to the fairies both by implication and confession as we see in the examples found across the 16th and 17th century Scottish Witchcraft trials. Of course, it must be acknowledged when discussing this material that the accounts given by these witches were obtained under duress, however, it is also worth noting the way that fairies were often used as a defence against accusations; when the accusers claimed the person consorted with demons the accused might respond by claiming they dealt with fairies instead. Witches and cunningfolk who learned from the fairies or were beholden to the Fairy Queen claimed to be approached during transitional social periods, as well as periods of crisis, such as Scottish witch Bessie Dunlop, tried in Edinburgh in 1576, who first met the Fairy Queen while Bessie was birthing a child and encountered the fairies again when her husband and child were very ill. Humans who already existed at the fringe of society or had been othered due to economic or social factors were common targets of fairy attention and fairies were often named as the source of esoteric knowledge, beings who appeared and taught these humans how to heal in order to give the human a viable career option. Fairy Queens also broke human boundaries relating to gender by giving knowledge and skill normally associated with women to men, as we see in the testimony of Andro Man of Aberdeen during his 1597 trial for witchcraft who credited the fairy Queen with teaching him all of the healing he knew (Purkiss, 2000).

Accused witch and cunningman Andro Man said of the Fairy Queen that she *"is very pleasant, and will be old and young when she pleases; she makes any king she pleases and lays with any she likes"*[11] expressing the idea not only that the true power lies with the Queen, who can make a king as she chooses, but also that she can and will take any lover she likes. Andro Man claimed to have been one of the Queen's lovers himself and to have fathered many children with her across 30 years (Wilby, 2006). Accused witch Margret Alexander, tried in 1647, said that the Fairy King was her lover, although she also said the experience was unpleasant for her and her account reflects many of the stereotypes found at the time of a witch's sexual union with the Devil, including the claim that his semen was cold (Henderson & Cowan, 2007). The conflation of the Fairy King and Christian Devil was relatively common in these accounts, although the Fairy Queen was viewed in a different light, not compared to a succubus or demon but to the majestic Queen of Heaven, despite the Fairy Queen's sexual nature and actions contrasting with the Virgin Mary's virtue and chastity.

Not all such unions between fairies and witches were as voluntary, however. Elspeth Reoch, tried in Orkney in 1616, and Isobell Strathaquin, of Aberdeen, tried in 1597, claimed they were required to have sex with a fairy man before being given any supernatural knowledge or skill (Henderson & Cowan, 2007). In Elspeth Reoch's case this was clearly not desirable to her as she initially refused, having just given birth to her first child, but was relentlessly harassed and kept awake for three days by the fairy until she finally agreed; she woke the following morning unable to speak (Wilby, 2006). In this we see a sharp contrast to the romantic tales of fairy love in Chapter 4, as here the witch's consent to the sexual encounter is not given after seduction or wooing but is reluctantly offered when no other option is acceptable to the amorous fairy and he has made refusal more unpleasant than agreement.

The Ballad Material

We've touched on some examples from the ballad material briefly throughout this text but here we need to take a longer look, to explore the way the ballads can illustrate the relationship between fairies and sex and humans and fairies. This section is, by necessity, not exhaustive nor is intended to reflect a deep dive into fairies in ballads, which would require nearly an entire book of its own. The intent here is to convey only the broad strokes of these songs and the concepts attached to them as they reflect the wider beliefs of their time.

The following four ballads all appear in *Child's 1882 English and Scottish Popular Ballads collection*; the fifth poem is from Goerge Douglas's *Scottish Fairy and Folk Tales,* circa 1900. I will include one version of each below but encourage those interested in exploring the material to go to the books referenced in order to see the range of lyrical variation. Many of the oldest versions of these ballads can be dated back to the early 1600s and are still known and sung today.

Tam Lin – Perhaps the most well-known fairy ballad is Tam Lin, which tells the story of a human woman, under various names, who goes to a forbidden fairy well and pays for the transgression with her virginity, a toll that the fairy knight who guards the well takes of maidens.[12] There are over a dozen older variants of the ballad and how consensual the sexual encounter is varies greatly between them, from the human woman being clearly an enthusiastic participant to equally clearly not consenting to it. Whatever version we are looking at the human woman falls pregnant and returns to the wood near the well, now seeking abortifacient herbs, only to encounter the fairy knight again. He confronts her about her desire to abort their child, then convinces her that he can be her husband, in the human world, if she has the courage to rescue him from the Fairy host. The bulk of the ballad tells the story of that rescue, as the protagonist waits at midnight for the fairy rade to pass by, pulls her lover off his horse, and holds him through multiple changes of form that the Fairy Queen inflicts to test her resolve. When she succeeds Tam Lin is turned back into a mortal man, as he had been a human once stolen by the Fairy Queen.

The sexuality in Tam Lin is dangerous and boundary crossing, not only in the possibly questionable consent but also in the choices made by the protagonist to go to the well knowing the toll that might be taken and in choosing to save her elfin lover. An added layer in this particular ballad is the proclaimed love, in some versions, that the Fairy Queen has for Tam Lin and her cursing the human protagonist for stealing him away.

This is version A from Child's 1882 collection:

O I forbid you, maidens a',
That wear gowd on your hair,
To come or gae by Carterhaugh,
For young Tam Lin is there.
There's nane that gaes by Carterhaugh
But they leave him a wad,
Either their rings, or green mantles,
Or else their maidenhead.
Janet has kilted her green kirtle
A little aboon her knee,
And she has broded her yellow hair
A little aboon her bree,
And she's awa to Carterhaugh
As fast as she can hie.

When she came to carterhaugh
Tam Lin was at the well,
And there she fand his steed standing,
But away was himsel.
She had na pu'd a double rose,
A rose but only twa,
Till upon then started young Tam Lin,
Says, Lady, thou's pu nae mae.
Why pu's thou the rose, Janet,
And why breaks thou the wand?
Or why comes thou to Carterhaugh
Withoutten my command?
"Carterhaugh, it is my own,
My daddy gave it me,
I'll come and gang by Carterhaugh,
And ask nae leave at thee."
Janet has kilted her green kirtle
A little aboon her knee,
And she has broded her yellow hair
A little aboon her bree,
And she is to her father's ha,
As fast as she can hie.
Four and twenty ladies fair
Were playing at the ba,
And out then came the fair Janet,
The flower among them a'.
Four and twenty ladies fair
Were playing at the chess,
And out then came the fair Janet,
As green as onie glass.
Out then spake an auld grey knight,
Lay oer the castle wa,
And says, Alas, fair Janet, for thee,
But we'll be blamed a'.

"Haud your tongue, ye auld fac'd knight,
Some ill death may ye die!
Father my bairn on whom I will,
I'll father none on thee."
Out then spak her father dear,
And he spak meek and mild,
"And ever alas, sweet Janet," he says,
"I think thou gaest wi child."
"If that I gae wi child, father,
Mysel maun bear the blame,
There's neer a laird about your ha,
Shall get the bairn's name.
"If my love were an earthly knight,
As he's an elfin grey,
I wad na gie my ain true-love
For nae lord that ye hae.
"The steed that my true love rides on
Is lighter than the wind,
Wi siller he is shod before,
Wi burning gowd behind."
Janet has kilted her green kirtle
A little aboon her knee,
And she has broded her yellow hair
A little aboon her bree,
And she's awa to Carterhaugh
As fast as she can hie.
When she came to Carterhaugh,
Tam Lin was at the well,
And there she fand his steed standing,
But away was himsel.
She had na pu'd a double rose,
A rose but only twa,
Till up then started young Tam Lin,
Says, Lady, thou pu's nae mae.

"Why pu's thou the rose, Janet,
Amang the groves sae green,
And a' to kill the bonny babe
That we gat us between?"
"O tell me, tell me, Tam Lin," she says,
"For's sake that died on tree,
If eer ye was in holy chapel,
Or christendom did see?"
"Roxbrugh he was my grandfather,
Took me with him to bide
And ance it fell upon a day
That wae did me betide.
"And ance it fell upon a day
A cauld day and a snell,
When we were frae the hunting come,
That frae my horse I fell,
The Queen o' Fairies she caught me,
In yon green hill do dwell.
"And pleasant is the fairy land,
But, an eerie tale to tell,
Ay at the end of seven years,
We pay a tiend to hell,
I am sae fair and fu o flesh,
I'm feard it be mysel.
"But the night is Halloween, lady,
The morn is Hallowday,
Then win me, win me, an ye will,
For weel I wat ye may.
"Just at the mirk and midnight hour
The fairy folk will ride,
And they that wad their true-love win,
At Miles Cross they maun bide."
"But how shall I thee ken, Tam Lin,
Or how my true-love know,

Amang sa mony unco knights,
The like I never saw?"
"O first let pass the black, lady,
And syne let pass the brown,
But quickly run to the milk-white steed,
Pu ye his rider down.
"For I'll ride on the milk-white steed,
And ay nearest the town,
Because I was an earthly knight
They gie me that renown.
"My right hand will be gloved, lady,
My left hand will be bare,
Cockt up shall my bonnet be,
And kaimed down shall my hair,
And thae's the takens I gie thee,
Nae doubt I will be there.
"They'll turn me in your arms, lady,
Into an esk and adder,
But hold me fast, and fear me not,
I am your bairn's father.
"They'll turn me to a bear sae grim,
And then a lion bold,
But hold me fast, and fear me not,
And ye shall love your child.
"Again they'll turn me in your arms
To a red het gand of airn,
But hold me fast, and fear me not,
I'll do you nae harm.
"And last they'll turn me in your arms
Into the burning gleed,
Then throw me into well water,
O throw me in with speed.
"And then I'll be your ain true-love,

I'll turn a naked knight,
Then cover me wi your green mantle,
And hide me out o sight."
Gloomy, gloomy was the night,
And eerie was the way,
As fair Jenny in her green mantle
To Miles Cross she did gae.
At the mirk and midnight hour
She heard the bridles sing,
She was as glad at that
As any earthly thing.
First she let the black pass by,
And syne she let the brown,
But quickly she ran to the milk-white steed,
And pu'd the rider down.
Sae weel she minded what he did say,
And young Tam Lin did win,
Syne covered him wi her green mantle,
As blythe's a bird in spring
Out then spak the Queen o Fairies,
Out of a bush o broom,
"Them that has gotten young Tam Lin
Has gotten a stately-groom."
Out then spak the Queen o Fairies,
And an angry woman was she,
"Shame betide her ill-far'd face,
And an ill death may she die,
For she's taen awa the bonniest knight
In a' my companie.
"But had I kend, Tam Lin," said she,
"What now this night I see,
I wad hae taen out thy twa grey een,
And put in twa een o tree."

Thomas the Rhymer – We also find this dangerous sexuality in the ballad of Thomas the Rhymer, where the Fairy Queen is, as Dunnigan describes her in *From Fairy Queens to Ogresses*:

> *Both idealized and feared...vividly associated with ideas and images of the sinful and demonic... and as [embodying] these simultaneous binaries and oppositions: vestiges of both Eve and the Virgin Mary in one version, and therefore a source of simultaneous redemption and damnation* (Dunnigan, 2016).

Thomas's taking of the Queen as his lover in the prose text, or the kiss he shares with her in the ballad, both place him in her power and put him into her service for seven years, demonstrating one less deadly but no less serious consequence for such interactions.

Thomas the Rhymer, as with the previously discussed prose version, tells the story of Thomas of Erceldoune and his abduction into Fairy by the Fairy Queen. The ballad version is much less overtly sexual than the prose tale, with only a kiss shared between the pair, but retains the wider theme of Thomas being taken away by the queen then returned with the gift of prophecy, or more precisely the gift of true speech. Thomas is not pleased with this stating that it will make his life much more difficult, but the queen is not swayed.

From Child's Collection:

> *True Thomas lay on Huntlie Bank,*
> *A ferlie he spied wi' his eye*
> *And there he saw a lady bright,*
> *Come riding down by Eildon Tree.*
> *Her shirt was o the grass-green silk,*
> *Her mantle o the velvet fyne*
> *At ilka tett of her horse's mane*

Hang fifty siller bells and nine.
True Thomas, he pulld aff his cap,
And louted low down to his knee
"All hail, thou mighty Queen of Heaven!
For thy peer on earth I never did see."
"O no, O no, Thomas," she said,
"That name does not belang to me;
I am but the queen of fair Elfland,
That am hither come to visit thee."
"Harp and carp, Thomas," she said,
"Harp and carp along wi' me,
And if ye dare to kiss my lips,
Sure of your bodie I will be."
"Betide me weal, betide me woe,
That weird shall never daunton me;"
Syne he has kissed her rosy lips,
All underneath the Eildon Tree.
"Now, ye maun go wi me," she said,
"True Thomas, ye maun go wi me,
And ye maun serve me seven years,
Thro weal or woe, as may chance to be."
She mounted on her milk-white steed,
She's taen True Thomas up behind,
And aye wheneer her bridle rung,
The steed flew swifter than the wind.
O they rade on, and farther on—
The steed gaed swifter than the wind—
Untill they reached a desart wide,
And living land was left behind.
"Light down, light down, now, True Thomas,
And lean your head upon my knee;
Abide and rest a little space,
And I will shew you ferlies three."
"O see ye not that narrow road,

So thick beset with thorns and briers?
That is the path of righteousness,
Tho after it but few enquires.
"And see not ye that braid braid road,
That lies across that lily leven?
That is the path to wickedness,
Tho some call it the road to heaven.
"And see not ye that bonny road,
That winds about the fernie brae?
That is the road to fair Elfland,
Where thou and I this night maun gae.
"But, Thomas, ye maun hold your tongue,
Whatever ye may hear or see,
For, if you speak word in Elflyn land,
Ye'll neer get back to your ain countrie."
O they rade on, and farther on,
And they waded thro rivers aboon the knee,
And they saw neither sun nor moon,
But they heard the roaring of the sea.
It was mirk mirk night, and there was nae stern light,
And they waded thro red blude to the knee;
For a' the blude that's shed on earth
Rins thro the springs o that countrie.
Syne they came on to a garden green,
And she pu'd an apple frae the tree:
"Take this for thy wages, True Thomas,
It will give the tongue that can never lie."
"My tongue is mine ain," True Thomas said;
"A gudely gift ye was gie to me!
I neither dought to buy nor sell,
At fair or tryst where I may be.
"I dought neither speak to prince or peer,
Nor ask of grace from fair ladye:"
"Now hold thy peace," the lady said,

"For as I say, so must it be."
He has gotten a coat of the even cloth,
And a pair of shoes of velvet green,
And till seven years were gane and past
True Thomas on earth was never seen.

The Elfin Knight – This ballad is the predecessor of the song 'Scarborough Faire' and tells the tale of a young girl who hears an elf knight blowing his horn on May Day and wishes that she could have him for her own. The elf appears at her side but immediately tries to convince her to release him, arguing that they are ill matched due to her age, which varies but in version D is given as nine years old. The girl argues back that she is old enough to wed as her younger sister just has:

She had no sooner these words said,
When that the knight came to her bed.
'Thou art over young a maid,' quoth he,
'Married with me thou il wouldst be.'
'I have a sister younger than I,
And she was married yesterday.
(Child, 1882)

He responds to her insistence by requesting she complete several impossible tasks to which she replies with a longer list of even more fantastical requests, including ploughing the earth with a thorn and threshing a crop in a shoe. In versions A and B the elf then tells her that he will not abandon his wife and children for her, while in later versions the girl tells him to return when he has completed the tasks and she will have his requests done as well.

The sexuality is fairly overt in this ballad, with the girl or young woman saying she wants the elf in her arms, and when he protests in version D she proclaims that her younger sister *'to the young men's bed has made bold'*. In both versions A and B when the elf eventually tells her that he will not leave his wife for her, she declares that she will keep her virginity and he can do what he will. Although this ballad is interesting in its own right due to the challenges each character issues the other, it also demonstrates the wider understanding of the inherent sexuality of elves, juxtaposed perhaps against the surprisingly ethical unwillingness of the elf to accept a relationship with a girl he deems too young.

Version A from Child's Collection:

My plaid awa, my plaid awa,
And ore the hill and far awa,
And far awa to Norrowa,
My plaid shall not be blown awa.
The elphin knight sits on yon hill,
    Ba, ba, ba, lilli ba
He blaws his horn both lowd and shril.
    The wind hath blown my plaid awa
He blowes it east, he blowes it west,
He blowes it where he lyketh best.
"I wish that horn were in my kist,
Yea, and the knight in my armes two."
She had no sooner these words said,
When that the knight came to her bed.
"Thou art over young a maid," quoth he,
"Married with me thou il wouldst be."
"I have a sister younger than I,
And she was married yesterday."
"Married with me if thou wouldst be,
A courtesie thou must do to me.
"For thou must shape a sark to me,
Without any cut or heme," quoth he.

"Thou must shape it knife-and-sheerlesse,
And also sue it needle-threedlesse."
"If that piece of courtesie I do to thee,
Another thou must do to me.
"I have an aiker of good ley-land,
Which lyeth low by yon sea-strand.
"For thou must eare it with thy horn,
So thou must sow it with thy corn.
"And bigg a cart of stone and lyme,
Robin Redbreast he must trail it hame.
"Thou must barn it in a mouse-holl,
And thrash it into thy shoes soll.
thou must winnow it in thy looff,
And also seck it in thy glove.
"For thou must bring it over the sea,
And thou must bring it dry home to me.
en thou hast gotten thy turns well done,
Then come to me and get thy sark then."
"I'l not quite my plaid for my life;
It haps my seven bairns and my wife."
*   The wind shall not blow my plaid awa*
"My maidenhead I'l then keep still,
Let the elphin knight do what he will."
*   The wind's not blown my plaid awa*

Lady Isabel and the Elf Knight – the much darker version of the theme found in The Elfin Knight, Lady Isobel and the Elf Knight also starts with a woman – an adult this time – hearing an elf horn blow on May Day and wishing for the elf as her lover. Lady Isobel's elf, however, is of a very different sort than the Elfin Knight; he appears in Isobel's room and forces her out, making her ride with him into the woods where he announces that he will kill her. She begs to be freed but he says that he has already killed seven kings' daughters and that she will be the eighth. She lures him into resting his head on her knee and lulls him to sleep before killing him with his own dagger. The sexual nature of their encounter is not explicit but her wish to have *"yen elf-knight to sleep in my bosom"* sets the initial tone and her final words that he is now laying there as a husband to the seven murdered princesses, as well as the way she lures him to sleep in her lap at the least imply a sexual union occurs or was intended.

Lady Isobel's Elf Knight is in sharp contrast to the more chivalrous and alluring elven lovers of other tales, but does align with the dangerous tales of female fairies who seduce and kill, perhaps offering some counterbalance to that view.

Version from Child's Collection:

Fair lady Isabel sits in her bower sewing,
    Refrain:Aye as the gowans grow gay
There she heard an elf-knight blawing his horn.
    Refrain:The first morning in May
"If I had yon horn that I hear blawing,
And yon elf-knight to sleep in my bosom."
This maiden had scarcely these words spoken,
Till in at her window the elf-knight has luppen.
"It's a very strange matter, fair maiden," said he,
"I canna blaw my horn but ye call on me.
"But will ye go to yon greenwood side?
If ye canna gang, I will cause you to ride."
He leapt on a horse, and she on another,
And they rode on to the greenwood together.
"Light down, light down, lady Isabel," said he,
We are come to the place where ye are to die.
"Hae mercy, hae mercy, kind sir, on me,
Till ance my dear father and mother I see."

"Seven king's-daughters here hae I slain,
And ye shall be the eight o them."
"O sit down a while, lay your head on my knee,
That we may hae some rest before that I die."
She stroakd him sae fast, the nearer he did creep,
Wi a sma charm she lulld him fast asleep.
Wi his ain sword-belt sae fast as she ban him,
Wi his ain dag-durk sae sair as she dang him.
"If seven king's-daughters here ye hae slain,
Lye ye here, a husband to them a'."

Faery Oak of Corriewater – In the 19th century poem 'The Faerie Oak of Corriewater' we see the youth, Elph Erving, taken into the Fairy Queen's service in exchange for a kiss. His sister tracks down the fairies where they are celebrating and tries to retrieve him, but it doesn't go as well as the similar rescue in Tam Lin; in this poem the sister's resolve fails when her brother is turned into fire and she is killed. Her brother remains in the service of the Fairy Queen afterwards.

The following is from Goerge Douglas's book *Scottish Folk and Fairy Tales*, currently in the public domain:

The small bird's head is under its wing,
The deep sleeps on the grass;
The moon comes out, and the stars shine down,
The dew gleams like the glass:
There is no sound in the world so wide,
Save the sound of the smitten brass,
With the merry cittern and the pipe
Of the fairies as they pass.
But oh! the fir maun burn and burn,
And the hour is gone, and will never return.

The green hill cleaves, and forth, with a bound,
Comes elf and elfin steed;
The moon dives down in a golden cloud,
The stars grow dim with dread;
But a light is running along the earth,
So of heaven's they have no need:
O'er moor and moss with a shout they pass,
And the word is spur and speed—
But the fire maun burn, and I maun quake,
And the hour is gone that will never come back.
And when they came to Craigyburnwood,
The Queen of the Fairies spoke:
"Come, bind your steeds to the rushes so green,
And dance by the haunted oak:
I found the acorn on Heshbon Hill,
In the nook of a palmer's poke,
A thousand years since; here it grows!"
And they danced till the greenwood shook:
But oh! the fire, the burning fire,
The longer it burns, it but blazes the higher.
"I have won me a youth," the Elf Queen said,
"The fairest that earth may see;
This night I have won young Elph Irving
My cupbearer to be.
His service lasts but for seven sweet years,
And his wage is a kiss of me."
And merrily, merrily, laughed the wild elves
Round Corrie's greenwood tree.
But oh! the fire it glows in my brain,
And the hour is gone, and comes not again.
The Queen she has whispered a secret word,
"Come hither, my Elphin sweet,
And bring that cup of the charmed wine,

Thy lips and mine to weet."
But a brown elf shouted a loud, loud shout,
"Come, leap on your courses fleet,
For here comes the smell of some baptised flesh,
And the sounding of baptised feet."
But oh! the fire that burns, and maun burn;
For the time that is gone will never return.
On a steed as white as the new-milked milk,
The Elf Queen leaped with a bound,
And young Elphin a steed like December snow
'Neath him at the word he found.
But a maiden came, and her christened arms
She linked her brother around,
And called on God, and the steed with a snort
Sank into the gaping ground.
But the fire maun burn, and I maun quake,
And the time that is gone will no more come back.
And she held her brother, and lo! he grow
A wild bull waked in ire;
And she held her brother, and lo! he changed
To a river roaring higher;
And she held her brother, and he became
A flood of the raging fire;
She shrieked and sank, and the wild elves laughed
Till the mountain rang and mire.
But oh! the fire yet burns in my brain,
And the hour is gone, and comes not again.
"O maiden, why waxed thy faith so faint,
Thy spirit so slack and slaw?
Thy courage kept good till the flame waxed wud,
Then thy might began to thaw;
Had ye kissed him frae 'mang us a'.
New bless the fire, the elfin fire,

That made thee faint and fa';
Now bless the fire, the elfin fire,
The longer it burns it blazes the higher."

In all of these ballads we see the sexual interplay between humans and elves or fairies playing out, sometimes with a happy ending and other times very much not. These songs reflect the culturally embedded understandings of these beings as both sexual in nature and potentially dangerous, but also show the wider assumptions about power and control which the fairies were believed to have. Additionally, it adds evidence to the argument for fairies acting inverse to human social and sexual mores: where humans are chaste, fairies are promiscuous; where human men hold power, we find Fairy Queens more powerful. The seducing elf lives in the woods and yet also easily invades the bedroom if a woman opens herself up to his invasion with the wrong wish. The Fairy Queen steals away mortal men she fancies and binds them to her service with a kiss.

Chapter 6

Victorian Fairies

We must not look at goblin men,
We must not buy their fruits:
Who knows upon what soil they fed
Their hungry thirsty roots?"
"Come buy," call the goblins
Hobbling down the glen.
Rosetti, 'Goblin Market'

The Victorian period ushered in a new understanding of fairies in wider Western culture breaking from the previous millennia of accounts as these ancient beings were re-imagined through the filter of the British and American middleclass imagination and dissected and explained through the burgeoning fields of folklore and psychology. This new iteration of fairies was influenced by diverse factors including the wider mores of the Victorians themselves and the colonialist and rationalist mindset often applied to cultural folklore (Silver, 1999). Up until the mid-1800's fairies in folklore and belief are ubiquitously morally ambiguous, socially transgressing, gendered, and sexual creatures which move freely in and out of human norms. In the 19th and early 20th century, however, fairies were depicted in mass media and fiction in increasingly childlike and innocent ways, although through this era they did retain something of the older viciousness, or a shadow of it, that could be previously and simultaneously found in culturally specific folklore. As Purkiss points out in her book *At the Bottom of the Garden* the depiction of fairies as innocent is difficult for modern audiences to properly interpret as it seems to include a great deal of underlying innuendo that may or may not have been intentional.

Rosetti's poem 'Goblin Market' perhaps typifies this with a story of sisters one of whom is seduced into eating goblin fruit only to waste away afterwards; literary critics, folklorists, and readers have interpreted this poem as everything from a sexual allegory to straightforward folklore with no clear answer as to whether the innocence of the young women is genuine or coded language meant to imply something else. In any interpretation of the poem gender roles and sex are intrinsically intertwined with the supernatural in the depiction of both the human girls and the goblin men, as Rossetti uses traditional folkloric themes to illustrate contemporary struggles:

> Beneath the surface layer of Rossetti's works, which relied on fantastic metamorphoses to liberate women from traditionally assigned feminine roles, serious social issues are discussed and satirised. Sexual and social victimisation of women are thus prevented through Rossetti's employment of the fantastic in her works. Transformation in Rossetti's stories, then, occurs as a sexual liberation standing against social Darwinism, gender inequality, dominant social roles and, in short, against essentialism. (Sari, 2017).

In folklore and folk belief, the fairies that do remain overtly sexualized in popular stories become dangerous in their sexuality which is often conflated with or directly connected to vampirism even among fairy women appearing with infants (Silver, 1999). While this period sees an overall gentling and infantilizing of fairies there nonetheless remains an undercurrent of deviance from human social norms, seen most clearly perhaps in the stories of female fairies who act in stark contrast to the rigid cultural expectations of women at the time. As Silver puts it:

> ...it is worth noting that the figures the collectors found most fascinating were the solitary, undomesticated, uncontrolled

fairy females who went where they wished and when they wished, inverting all human laws of family and propriety. (Silver, 1999)

Fairy brides were a common example of this, beings who defied the standard expectations for women of the time as demur and fragile by embodying wilderness and carnal urges. Whether swan maidens or selkie wives they were wild women at heart, and even marriage to a human husband could only tame them temporarily. This also allowed the folklorists of the era to lean into stereotypes of women as closer to nature and to irrationality, inherently closer to sexuality and less able to control their own urges (Silver, 1999). As the fairies more generally were being diminished into the fodder of children's nurseries, the fairy brides and predatory fairy women were drawing comparisons with everything the society of the time saw as flawed in human women.

The overt sexuality of fairies outside those exceptions though was quickly subdued and exchanged for a twee innocence that came to permeate the subject, just as the powerful magic that had carried the fairy host aloft was exchanged for fragile insect wings. This was not the first radical re-envisioning of fairies nor will it be the last, as they have always been fluid and changeable across history. Across time the male aelf became female, the human-sized fairy became miniature, the fairy who brought ill luck and death became a gentle guardian of the flowers. Change is one of the few constants of fairy belief, paired perhaps with the idea that has persisted since Chaucer's time that the fairies are perpetually leaving yet never gone.

While much of the change in understanding fairies can be laid at the feet of the Victorian attempt to, as Purkiss puts it, *"have fairies, but not Queen Mab"* there were other influences as well, notably Theosophy, which rewrote the fairies far more radically than Victorian popular culture had done. Theosophy was founded in the late 1880's by madame Helena Blavatsky as a spirituality that incorporated various religious beliefs with assorted esoteric ones. According to Blavatsky fairies were nature spirits who in turn were elemental spirits, a type of being that existed below physical incarnation but were working towards achieving it, with an ultimate goal of becoming human (Blavatsky, 1893). These spirits are incapable of physical manifestation, are not individualized, and require human input to have even an intangible form (Theosophy World, 2023). They are, effectively, spirits that are shaped by human interaction into the beings we know from folklore but without that input exist in an undifferentiated, unformed state. Theosophy impacted the views of some of the people who are famous for writing about or depicting culture specific fairies, including WB Yeats and AE Russell, and so many of the ideas put forward by Blavatsky have found their way to wider audiences, often subtly. Theosophy also reinforces the idea of fairies as innocent beings, because through this view they are too unevolved to grasp higher concepts such as morality and are incapable of intentional maliciousness (Theosophy World, 2023). This aspect of belief was likely reflecting the wider Victorian ideas of fairies as childlike.

The infantilization of fairies was a reflection of cultural factors at play among the middle and upper-class Victorians and went hand in hand with the romanticization of the natural world and wilderness. This period moved popular understandings of fairies in England and the US away from the dangerous and into an idealized embodiment of the child, seeing childhood as a period of pure innocence (Purkiss, 2000). Fairies became children, both sweet and tempestuous, and by extension the purview of children, beings who existed not in folk belief but in a naïve imagination, populating storybooks and playtime.

This overt de-sexualization was neither complete nor all encompassing, as we have already seen with the fairy brides discussed above, but it was effective nonetheless. While there were some fears during this time that fairies wouldn't be tamed by association with children but that children would be sexualized by associating them with fairies, the wider result was to render fairies into winged children who existed in that shadowy realm before maturity (Purkiss, 2000).

Artistic depictions of fairies become both more revealing, tending to show these beings nude, and also more childlike as may be seen in the early 20th century art of Cicely Mary Barker's immensely popular flower fairies. The overt sexuality that had been the hallmark of fairies is subsumed by a more subtle sexuality or even asexuality. Suggs in *Fairies: A Dangerous History* discusses various specific examples of this across the 19th and 20th centuries noting the ephemeral colour palette ubiquitous across the works and the way that the images retain some otherworldliness while losing any sense of danger, noting that the imagery moved into the 20th century with a distinctly androgynous tone. The sexuality and sexual symbolism in fairy artwork become subtly ingrained and most often delineates women from men, showing fairy women as quietly, irresistibly seductive (Purkiss, 2000).

Lurking in the softened, childlike Victorian fairies we find a deep misogyny which renders even the now ingénue female fairy an alluring figure which could lead girls into amorality, should they be tempted to follow that fairy onto the stage (Purkiss, 2000). The well-known figure of Tinkerbell in the book and play is a thoroughly childlike fairy yet even she plays out the jealousy of an adult woman, trying to have her rival killed to keep all of Peter's attention for herself. The cultural desire to suppress the sexuality of fairies to render them fit for children served only to redefine it and hide it.

So thoroughly did the term fairy come to be associated with childhood and fancy dress in contrast to the previous fear and awe that made even speaking the word taboo that Kipling, writing towards the end of this time period, had his character Puck proclaim:

[fairies] are made-up things the People of the Hills have never heard of—little buzzflies with butterfly wings and gauze petticoats, and shiny stars in their hair, and a wand like a school-teacher's cane for punishing bad boys and rewarding good ones...Can you wonder that the People of the Hills don't care to be confused with that painty-winged, wand-waving, sugar-and-shake-your-head set of impostors? Butterfly wings, indeed! (Kipling, 1906).

This thorough excoriation of the Victorian fairy, put in the mouth of a famously folkloric being, illustrated the contrasting views on the subject that had come to exist by the early 20th century. On one hand the older, culturally ingrained views which permeated myth, literature, and folklore to that point, and on the other hand the sanitized, disempowered, and de-sexualized fairies which cavorted across children's literature and art.

Chapter 7

Modern Fairies

The song speaks of Janet, and Margaret, and Marjorie May,
And a fool might think that that I was the bane of one woman
*   with many names,*
That different minstrels changed the name of my savior to
*   flatter*
The daughter of each house where he sang the tune, but I was
*   never saved:*
There are ghosts of old autumns here, and bones white as pearl,
*   yellow as ivory*
Lay in drifts like snow under the oaks, tangled together like
*   wood stacked for*
Beltane's fire. I was never born mortal man, never christened
*   like my brides...*
Jennifer Lawrence, 'Tam Lin's Garden', 2009

20th Century

Following the Victorian era into the 20th century, the
conceptualization of fairies continued to modify in Western
culture, influenced by theosophy and the new age movement's
understanding of fairies as simultaneously elemental beings[13]
and manifested spirits of the natural world. These views are
found across the array of written fairy material by authors
including William Butler Yeats, AE Russell, Lady Wilde, and
folklorists' interpretations of fairies, such as we see in Evans-
Wentz's seminal work *The Fairy Faith in Celtic Countries*. The
infamous Cottingley Fairy incident combined the Victorian
miniaturizing and infantilizing of fairies with the growing
view of fairies as spirits of nature and the purview of children.

Moving into the later 19th and early 20th century and then solidifying in the later 20th century fairies were increasingly understood outside traditional folklore as genderless and non-physical beings. In the late 20th and 21st century anecdotal accounts reflect these newer views, with people discussing encounters with fairies that are genderless, express no sexuality, and may even be formless.[14] 20th and 21st century authors of fiction and pagan material would solidify this trend in the public mind with taxonomies and descriptions of fairies that explicitly defined them as androgynous and asexual, or leaned into the earlier Victorian childlike depictions establishing the understanding of fairies now found across mass media. Most modern movie depictions of fairies, particularly those aimed at younger audiences, follow this approach.[15] This view has come to dominate across some demographics, while the older traditional view remains in others, creating a tension between the two antithetical interpretations and confusion about the nature, gender, and sexuality of fairies more generally.

Tolkien's Elves

With the exercise of the power (of generation), the desire soon ceases, and the mind turns to other things...they have many other urges of body and of mind which their nature urges them to fulfil. Tolkien, 'Laws and Customs of the Eldar', 1993

One surprising influence on how the subject of elves/fairies and sex came to be understood is JRR Tolkien. His books, from the 1937 *Hobbit* through to the posthumous works still being released today, have had a profound impact on modern fantasy and by extension on how these beings are perceived outside of fiction. The movie adaptions of the stories, beginning with the 2001 *Fellowship of the Ring* have also played a role in this, particularly in how elves are envisioned. The material on elves in the *Lord of the Ring* trilogy and the *Silmarillion* have been especially impactful, not only shaping a wider understanding of elves but also inspiring an entire religion based around elvish spiritual beliefs called Tië eldaliéva.

Tolkien's elves were heavily based on Anglo-Saxon, Norse, and Celtic mythology, although in later revisions of his work he tended to drop the more tempestuous, dangerous aspect of the mythic beings and instead leaned into the idea of them as beautiful, wise, and powerful beings who exceeded humans in skills and strength. Drawing from the Anglo-Saxon aelfe, discussed in Chapter 2, Tolkien's elves were androgynous beings, the men as beautiful as the women and the women as strong and fast as the men, with childbearing being the critical difference between the two (Tyellas, 2009). Unlike the Ango-Saxon aelfe, however, Tolkien's elves were not overtly gendered in their roles nor were they sexually aggressive, particularly towards humans. No one would confuse the elves of the *Lord of the Rings* with incubi. Until the recent surge in romantic and erotic stories featuring elves (discussed in the next section) many other fantasy writers of the 20th century followed Tolkien's lead in approaching the subject of elves and sex, keeping the characters almost chaste and focusing on their wisdom and skill rather than any sexual allure.

The elves of Tolkien's books are sexual but only within the confines of marriage; in point of fact the act of sexual union is what initiates marriage among them and Tolkien explicitly associates sex, marriage, and the begetting of children (Tyellas, 2009). He is unsurprisingly heteronormative in his stories but is surprisingly sex positive, always describing consensual sex as a good thing. Conception for elves is a conscious act, so that there is no concept of unwanted children or accidental pregnancies, nor of birth control.

Tolkien was a devout catholic and although his work is undeniably pagan in many respects, particularly the story of the world's creation and the elves, Tolkien understood it to be a Christian series, saying: "*The Lord of the Rings is of course a fundamentally religious and Catholic work; unconsciously so at first, but consciously in the revision*" (Haas, 2004). This religious bias may perhaps manifest in part through this depiction of elves who reflect Tolkien's own ideals, as well as the wider approach to sex and love in his books which emphasizes the sanctity and importance of marriage and of sex only within that context (Tyellas, 2003; 2009).

It is interesting to note that although Tolkien's own intentions with his elves may have been idealized, Catholic, and heteronormative his work is often read through a queer lens. This subject is discussed at length in the essays in *Tolkien and Alterity* edited by Vaccaro and Kisor, with Kisor's opening essay 'Queer Tolkien: A Bibliographical Essay on Tolkien and Alterity' establishing the arguments for and against such readings and exploring the concepts anchored around a queer view of Tolkien's work. A queer reading of Tolkien tends to focus on the relationship between Sam and Frodo more than on Tolkien's elves, but can be extended outside that pair to include all the characters; as the article 'What Tolkien Officially Said About Elf Sex' notes, Tolkien never wrote about his elves being gay but he also never said they weren't.

A notable change in the view of elves began to occur with the release of the first movie adaptation of the books, with the movies being noted for their queer subtext and giving rise to endless fanfiction that depicted the elves as highly sexual, leaning into both original slash fic[16] and re-envisioning of the source text and films. This allowed the elves to be seen as overtly sexual in ways that the source material doesn't depict them and, somewhat ironically, returned the elves to a sexuality that is closer to that of Tolkien's own source material in the myths and folklore.

For our purposes here it is enough to note that Tolkien's elves into the 21st century have moved well out of Tolkien's original texts and that the diverse views and understandings of high fantasy elves has grown to reflect as full a range of gender and sexual expression as can be found within – and even beyond – Western culture. This adaptation can be seen in the way that the androgynous, nearly asexual elves of mid-20th century high fantasy have morphed into the diverse range of gender and sexuality expressed across 21st century fantasy genres. However, for those influenced by Tolkien's works, without the modern fan fiction lens, and who lean more into the wider new age/post-Theosophy understanding of fairies, these beings remain largely asexual.

Urban Fantasy

Another factor which effects modern perceptions of fairy sexuality has been urban fantasy, which frequently influences active belief outside of cultures that have living fairy beliefs. Fairies have steadily gained popularity in urban fantasy over the last 40 years and are found across a wide range of series and single books seeking to depict modern settings with supernatural elements. Late 20th century depictions of fairies in the nascent genre of urban fantasy drew on older folklore and wider cultural motifs around fairies, portraying them in ways that were different from but heavily based in folklore, but as the genre developed and grew this understanding changed as well altering the understanding of these beings in new directions. The depiction of fairies, of various specific types, moved away from being seen as powerful, obscure, and dangerous beings and increasingly came to be seen as humanized, sympathetic, and even romantic figures.

There has been an increasing emphasis on romance between human or partially human protagonists and fairies since the late 1990s and early 2000s. While the wider idea of fairy-human romances is far from new, tracing back over a thousand years in written material, the fairy romances of urban fantasy are distinctly different in tone and narrative from the older texts. Medieval and early modern fairy romances depict heavily contractual relationships wherein the human is obligated to abide by specific rules set by the fairy lover in order to retain their romantic and sexual favour (Spyra, 2020). In contrast modern urban fantasy that incorporates romance or sex between fairies and humans includes emotions as key factors and uses sex and romance to define the fairy characters in different ways.

In the modern fairy romances of urban fantasy, the romance and sex between humans and fairies is indistinguishable from the sex and romance found in other romance sub-genres, following a predictable pattern of characters meeting, falling in love, overcoming obstacles to prove that love, and earning true love or a soul mate as a reward (RWA, 2024). In contrast the fairy romances of earlier periods were distinctly different from human romances, hinging heavily on contractual agreements between the two parties displayed through both physical and symbolic gift giving in which often the fairy lover themselves was both the gift and the gift giver and the human, unable as a non-magical being to respond adequately in kind, was instead put in the position of accepting specific prohibitions in exchange (Spyra, 2020).

The current understanding of fairies based in modern fiction is the culmination of the wider pattern of romanticizing these beings and of anthropomorphizing them that can be found in literature and among those coming from outside traditions of belief but seeking to revive those beliefs. Dr. Sabina Magliocco discusses these trends in her papers 'Taming the Fae' and 'Reconnecting to Everything' noting particularly the affects among neopagans who seek to actively incorporate fairies into their belief systems and who are more prone to looking at literature as a primary source and of blending literature with folk belief to form a syncretic view. In the first paper she argues that oral traditions are intrinsically connected to literary ones in these groups and that the gentler Victorian and Edwardian views of fairies directed the understanding of these beings away from the more dangerous ones of traditional folklore (Magliocco, 2019). In the latter paper she discusses the intentional revival of fairy beliefs which is described as *"filtered through literary and ethnographic portrayals of fairies, and romanticized because these narratives reflect a longing for an imagined past"* (Magliocco, 2018). The fairies of these new beliefs then are formed from diverse sources across media, from modern fiction, the folkloresque, and older folklore, and amalgamated to create a unique understanding filtered through mainstream Western culture which repurposes the fairy, particularly the dangerous ones, as lovers.

The Innocent Fairy

In conceptualizing the evolution of fairies across folklore and culture into the 20th and 21st centuries there is a paradigm shift from understanding fairies as intrinsically gendered and sexual and into viewing fairies as representing innocence and a childlike spirit. This can be particularly tied to the Victorian interpretation of fairies but is notable because it continues to reflect the inverse of human societal norms and also has allowed for a new form of human imitation of fairy. As modern Western culture began to restrict the role of men away from creativity and emotional expression those men who followed artistic paths were increasingly seen as irresponsible, naïve, and perhaps even feminine and therefore associated by implication with the fairies who themselves came to represent the unbridled and uninhibited joy of childhood (Suggs, 2019). Increasingly into the 20th century fairies and children became intertwined, not in the dangerous way of past folklore which attributed child abduction and changelings to fairies, but in a whimsical sense that viewed fairies as a type of eternal child-like spirit. Children costumed in wings played the part of fairies in the theatre and at fancy dress parties. Literature and poetry of the time depicted fairies in the same ways and they became the purview of children of the middle class, reflecting the idyllic worldview advocated there with its romanticism of nature and universal goodness. Suggs notes that by the late 1920's human children might be referred to as fairies in an endearing way, indicating the depth of the crossover, and describes several English social groups or clubs for children which allowed a child to become a fairy associate. Fairies became the property of these children and were off limits to adults deemed too mature for such fancy. This predictably led to adults who took on the mantle of fairy – or sometimes the literal wings – to retain such childlike innocence in defiance of the social norms dictating they reject this whimsy for rationality and responsibility. Leading into the 21st century this trend has not weakened and we may find professional fairies as well as those who take on the role of fairy precisely because it goes against the wider expectation of adult behaviours and allows for an embracing of innocence (Suggs, 2019). In this way the existing pattern of humans associating with and mimicking fairies' sexuality and deviance has been maintained in a new guise which now rejects wider cultural sexualization and maturity and clings to the qualities of post-Victorian fairies epitomized by childlike innocence and purity.

Moving further into the 21st century we are presented with popculture fairies that exist on very different ends of a sexual spectrum. The two sharply contrasting views of fairy sexuality exist simultaneously, with the asexual childlike fairy next to the romantic, sexualized fictional figure. Neither aligns with the fairies of the past or with the fairies that have existed and still exist across active folk beliefs linked to specific cultures, but both are aspects of folk belief today.

Chapter 8

Fairies, Humans, and Deviance

Across historic accounts and even into modern popular culture fairies are known for transgressing human social norms. As Briggs succinctly puts it *'(t)he fairies, as one would expect, have no special bias towards respectability...'* (Briggs, 1967). This can be seen in the stories of fairy wives who would cry at births and laugh at funerals, the Baobhan Sìth of Scottish folklore, who human men would find in the deep woods and who would seduce and kill those same men, and the English tales of Robin Goodfellow that place him in the role of domestic spirit. Fairies cross the barrier between life and death, stealing living humans to enhance their own numbers and having seemingly dead humans among their ranks. When humans limit themselves to rigid structured dancing the fairies dance wildly and unrestrained in the night. While humans focus on industry and work the fairies of ballads and literature spend their time in leisurely activities including riding, hunting, and dancing (Wimberly, 1965). In the movie *Fern Gully* when humans have lost touch with the natural world and focus only on consumption fairies appear as ecological warriors defending the nature that is being destroyed and teaching its value. These examples show not only the contrasting nature of the fairies compared to humans but also the ways in which the fairies often directly contradict human behaviours. As Yeats said in *Celtic Twilight,* they are beings of unmixed emotions of *'untiring joys and sorrows'*, and this perhaps explains why the fairies of folklore engage with humans either through passion or hatred and why they are so quick to substitute human social norms for those that rule the world of Fairy. They bless and curse on their own whim and following their own standards, rewarding those they take a liking to with blessings and cruelly punishing those who offend them or commit even the smallest breach of fairy etiquette. As Narvaez says in his article 'The Social Function of Fairylore':

> ...fairies [in] social consciousness, therefore, yields at least a double image: one being that fairies constitute a foreign, external, challenging, "other" society ("them, "the gentry"); the second image being that of fairies as intimate ("we are the fairies children"), domestic, local ("the good neighbours") provocateurs. (Narveaz, 1991).

Fairies are also strongly connected, across folklore, with humans who break social boundaries and defy social norms. Fairies were most prone to steal or teach humans who were in periods of social liminality, most often birth, marriage, childbed, illness, or death (Purkiss, 2000). These transitional periods represented a weakening of the normally rigid social expectations of gender and behaviour and were thus times of danger and potential social aberration. Accounts of witches and cunningfolk who learned from the fairies or were beholden to the Fairy Queen claimed to be approached during these periods, as well as periods of crisis, such as Scottish witch Bessie Dunlop who was approached during childbirth by the Fairy Queen and again by the fairies when her husband and child were very ill. Other fairy favourites were humans who already existed at the fringe of society or had been othered due to economic or social factors. Ann Jefferies, for example, a young woman much entangled with fairies in 17th century Cornwall, was said to be unusually bold and daring and described by author Regina Buccola as "[refusing] to conform to social standards governing gendered behavior even before she was under fairy tutelage" (Buccola, 2006).

The strong association between fairies as boundary breachers and with humans on the social margins is also used by humans to excuse their own transgressions, leaning into the cultural acceptance of fairies' deviance as existing outside human social norms. Narvaez in his article 'Newfoundland Berry Pickers "In the Fairies"' concludes that fairies and stories of illicit encounters with fairies could have offered acceptable justification for social deviance within the society and saved the human involved from bearing any shameful consequences. Individuals, particularly witches, who lived outside or on the margins of human society were often connected to the fairies both by implication and confession. Additionally, fairies have been associated historically with groups of humans who broke social norms. This is perhaps clearest in examples of people rebelling against political oppression who would refer to themselves as servants of the fairies or even as the Fairy King and Queen. In England in the 14th and 15th centuries there were several rebellions led by people claiming such, including one very popular leader who fashioned himself the *'Queen of the feyre'* and dressed in women's clothes (Green, 2016; Purkiss, 2000). During this same time period there were also groups of men in England who protested against their lords by poaching deer under the guise of serving the fairies or being servants of the Queen of fairies (Purkiss, 2000). Purkiss suggests several explanations for why humans might take on the mantle of fairy servants while rebelling against oppressive human systems, including that the Fairy Queen may have represented a social inversion that would justify such rebellion. This is in line with the wider concept of fairies existing outside a human moral code and free of attached moral judgments, allowing humans who take on the mantle of fairies or fairy associates to also have some of that freedom through that connection.

Fairies were symbols of power outside human society, beings who existed beyond the clear moral order and who were ambiguous in their affiliations, neither clearly good or clearly bad. It has been and still is common in folklore across Ireland, the UK and into diasporic areas of Canada for fairies to be viewed as neither angels nor demons but a third class of being trapped in between the others and outside of the explicit morality of either god or the devil. This liminal positioning of fairies as interacting with humans but exempt in many respects from human moral expectations allowed for fairies in both literature and folklore to defy human social mores without wholesale rejection of their presence and influence. By extension humans who actively associated themselves with fairies or who were associated with them by their communities enjoyed a reflection of that protection as well, at least within those communities.

Chapter 9

Marriage to the Other

Until one bore Bridget his bride
Away from the merry dance.

He bore her away in his arms,
The handsomest young man there,
And his neck and his breast and his arms
Were drowned in her long dim hair.
Yeats, 'The Stolen Bride', 1893

Modern understandings of fairy and human relationships are complex but often reflect post-Victorian views of fairies as androgynous or childlike and asexual. This has led some people to assume that fairies would have no concept of marriage, nor a need for it, and for assumptions that there are no accounts of fairy marriages in folklore. This chapter will begin by exploring the older folklore, then dissecting the concept as it manifests across sources, before looking at modern iterations occurring primarily among neopagans. I'll note that I'm going to take a two-pronged approach here and address fairies as a specific group through mostly folklore and literature and secondarily the wider subject of the Good Folk across Western Europe. The waters get muddy here as the term fairy often has an ambiguous use in the source material, appearing as both a general term and one for a particular being; for our purposes here both the general and specific will be discussed.

First, I suppose we must define marriage as it will be used here; in this context we will be using the term to describe a committed relationship between two specific beings in which they or the narrator either explicitly use the term married or use the terms 'husband', 'wife', 'groom', 'bride', etc.. This relationship may or may not be monogamous and may or may not be permanent,[17] but is marked by the specific language used to describe it in the sources indicating that the couple in question were understood to be married within the context of that source.

I. Marriage with Fairies

Evidence of fairies getting or being married to other fairies as well as marrying humans can be found across folk belief. As Gibson rightly puts it *"One of the commonest features of fairy mythology is the marriage between a human-being and a fairy"* (Gibson, 1955). It is a folklore motif called the 'fairy bride' although we also find human brides with fairy grooms. Some families claim ancestry that traces back to fairies or other specific types of Otherworldly beings, both through marriage and without it, and stories of fairy spouses can be found across Europe.

Fairies marrying fairies is usually a detail mentioned within a wider story, and we are rarely given any profound insight via folklore into the practical aspects of this concept. Often marriages between human and fairy don't last and just as often they end badly, usually through an action on the human's part, however, there are some accounts of cross-species marriages that do end well, often with the human going into the world of Fairy. Below I will share a series of examples that illustrate these points, first addressing beings specifically named as fairies in the source and secondly where the term is used to translate other words into English.

- In van Zatzikhoven's 12th century 'Lancelet' we are told a story of the Arthurian knight Lancelot[18] who weds the fairy Iblis. She remains his faithful wife after he leaves her and he marries another and she accepts him back when he returns, after which the two have four children together. The story is German, based on French sources (at least allegedly) of British myth. One might note that Lancelet while human was fostered by the fairy Lady of the Lake so did have pre-existing ties to the world of Fairy before meeting Iblis.

- Shakespeare's Oberon and Titania are described as the King and Queen of Fairyland together, refer to each other as 'my lady' and 'my lord' and are if not outright said to be married, heavily implied in context to be so.
- In 'Ogier the Dane' Ogier is a human who is given six blessings by the fairies at his birth, the sixth of which is the love of a fairy woman. The end of the story finds him finally accepting her love and her offer of immortality as he goes off with her to Avalon.
- An anecdotal account from the Orkneys mentions a man who fell asleep on a fairy hill and was awakened by a beautiful fairy woman who he took as his wife. He already had a human wife but that didn't appear to be an issue. The man and his fairy wife had three daughters together. (Towrie, 2022)
- Duachas.ie contains an account of a fairy wedding, the story going that a human man was on his way home when he met a fairy man who invited him into a fairy fort, saying they were celebrating a wedding. The man entered and saw 'the fairy bride' playing music on a golden harp (Dúchas v1003 p 309)
- In most iterations of the 'fairy midwife' stories (which is indeed a motif in itself) the woman who the midwife is called to assist and who the fairy man calls his wife is recognized as a human woman thought to have died or gone missing.
- Lady Wilde recounts the tale of a young man who was taken into fairy and whose family hired a specialist, a fairy doctor, to recover him. After a week of effort, the

young man's spirit was said to appear before a crowd, summoned by the fairy doctor, and he asked to be left where he was with his fairy bride.

- In the Welsh tale of the Physicians of Myddfai a human man succeeds in courting and marrying a Gwairg Annwn, or Lake Maiden, although as we are told her agreement has a catch: *"and after some persuasion she consented to become his bride, on condition that they should only live together until she received from him three blows without a cause"*. The two are happily married for years until he does, indeed, give her three blows without cause and she disappears back into the lake.

- In Irish mythology the human[19] protagonist, Fionn, finds and marries a woman of the sidhe named Sadb, although she is later turned into a deer.

- In folklore its said that Fionn and Sadb's son, the half-sidhe/half-human Oisín was taken to Tír na nÓg by the sidhe woman Niamh; the two married according to popular versions of the tale and had two children before Oisín left to visit Ireland where he met his end.

- The ballad of the Elfin Knight tells the story of a young girl who hears an elf blowing his horn on May Day morning and wishes to have him for herself. When he appears in her room, he fairly quickly proclaims that she is too young to marry him. Later in the ballad he says that he has a wife already.

- In Thomas of Erceldoune Thomas's Queen of Elfland is married to the King of Fairy (or the Devil depending on the version).

- Selkies[20] are well-known to have relationships with humans although the male selkies are less commonly said to marry. Female selkies, however, feature prominently in stories as seal-wives who marry a human fisherman after their sealskin is stolen by him.

- Grimm relates a tale of an elf woman who entered a house and became the wife of a man living there and bore him four children before disappearing back as she'd come.
- In 17th century London a man named Goodwin Wharton was much involved with fairies, with the aid of a cunningwoman named Mary Parrish, and his personal journal noted that he was married to the Queen of Fairies[21] by her (Timbers, 2016).

Looking at the evidence there are some general conclusions we can reach, besides the fact that fairies do indeed marry both other fairies and sometimes humans. Firstly, marriage for fairies seems to have roughly the same purpose as for humans, either a commitment based in love or a union to achieve a goal (often reproduction). Also, as with humans, marriage for fairies is a diverse and varied concept that we see including both fidelity (the Elfin Knight didn't want another lover as he already has a wife) as well as what we may term ethical non-monogamy (the Orkney anecdote) and infidelity (Thomas the Rhymer). We also find examples of both happy marriages (Niamh and Oisín) as well as unhappy ones (selkie wives). Secondly marriage for fairies, unlike for humans, seems a much more contractual and reciprocal affair even when love is involved; fairies operate with distinct rules which they must follow even when they don't want to. An example of this might be the man who married the Lake Maiden – while the marriage seemed happy and loving she warned him she would leave if he struck her needlessly three times and when that happened, she did so. Similarly, we see in some accounts of selkie wives the idea that they did love their human husband but once the sealskin is found they must leave even if they don't want to; these are the stories where the selkie lingers as a seal and helps the husband fish. It is likely these prohibitions and rules reflect an effort by the fairy to equalize the relationship, to bridge the power gap between themselves and the human, by putting a requirement on the human to prove their dedication (Spyra, 2020). It is also possible that this is simply an aspect of fairy marriage and applies equally to marriage between fairies. We see a range of such prohibitions across stories from the aforementioned three strikes, to the human not being allowed to speak of the fairy to others, to the hidden sealskin. Gibson also notes that human-fairy marriages usually include specific features including a reluctance on the part of the fairy, prohibitions given by the fairy, and a taking back of anything given by the fairy, including children, when she leaves (Gibson, 1955).

II. Patterns

Having established that marriage was a common feature of stories involving fairies let's look at some patterns we can note within that wider concept particularly of the Good Folk marrying humans. I think this can help us further explore the idea of marriage with fairies and may be useful for those seeking to understand the concept.

Two Types of Marriage

Looking across the folklore one thing that quickly becomes evident is that marriage with fairies can be broken down into two rough categories: forced marriages and voluntary marriages.

Forced marriages occur both when a human captures an Otherworldly being or when a human is captured although generally it is a woman being captured no matter which version is in play. The Stolen Bride motif is based on the idea of a human woman being taken by an Otherworldly suitor to be married in the world of Fairy[22] for example, and can be found across both folklore and anecdotal accounts. The human woman is usually thought to be dead by her family but sometimes is able to communicate with a relative or her husband – if she were already married – and may or may not subsequently be rescued.

In the case of a fairy woman being taken as a spouse they are usually trapped in some way so that they cannot return to their own world and must marry the human who trapped them; selkies having their sealskins stolen, for example, or Maran who could be trapped if the knothole she entered through was blocked (Ashliman, 2005). John Rhys relates a story wherein a human man sees a group of fairies dancing and seizes one of the women out of the group, bringing her back to his home where he eventually persuades her to marry him (Rhys, 1901). In those examples the Otherworldly wife would immediately flee her human husband if she found a way to undo the magic holding her – the selkie must find her hidden sealskin and the mare must find and unblock the knothole through which she'd entered. A human taken and married into the Otherworld can only hope for one chance at rescue, usually during a fairy procession through the mortal world, and if that fails is trapped forever with their new spouse. We do see at least one example, in the ballad of the Elfin Knight, of a human woman (or girl) who tries to trap an elf into marriage; although she ultimately fails it does suggest that there were cases involving men as the captured spouse.

Voluntary marriages, similarly, occur with both combinations of partners. In the Echtra Nera and the Echtra Condla we see human men who gain fairy wives with the consent of the wife; in Connla's case the fairy woman goes to great lengths to convince Connla to return to her world with her, while in Nera's case the fairy wife is given to him by a Fairy King but nonetheless seems to be happy with the situation, providing Nera with essential advice throughout the story and bearing him a son. There is also an anecdotal account in Lady Wilde's work of a young human man taken by the sidhe who refuses to be rescued because he is happy with his fairy wife. The Welsh tale of the Physicians of Myddfai features a Lake Maiden who chooses to wed a human man after he successfully courts her and the Orkney tale of the

Great Silkie of Sule Skerry tells of a human woman who weds a selkie man. In Jean d'Arras tales of Melusine we see both Melusine and her mother Perryne choosing to marry human men out of apparent affection for them. In these cases, both partners are willing participants in the marriage through choice not coercion and often seem to feel some genuine love for the other person within the context of the story.

How This Happens

How a human gets into a marriage with a fairy across the folklore generally occurs in one of three ways: the human is compelled by the fairy, the human compels the fairy, or the human and fairy meet and choose to marry. In cases where the human is compelled by the fairy it is usually what we might classify as an abduction: there are multiple examples of this across Irish folklore, where a person (usually a woman) is kidnapped by the Sidhe and taken into the Otherworld to marry one of the Good Folk. In cases where the human is compelling the fairy they either use magic or steal a magical item from the fairy; the girl who hears an elf blowing his horn on May Day morning and wishes for him as her husband is an example, where the elf appears to be compelled to do as she wishes against his own will. The fairy woman in the lai of Graelent is another example, where Graelent steals the fairy woman's clothing while she bathes then refuses to return them until she consents to give him the two things he wants most: her presence and her love. In the third case the meeting and marriage are more along what might be considered typical lines although the speed that things occur in is usually swift – in most stories where both partners are willing, they often meet and marry quickly.

Gain and Loss

Another notable pattern that we must discuss is that in all of the examples we find of mixed species marriages, humans and

Other, one partner must inevitably – by choice or force – give up their own world for the length of the marriage. This is not as simple as choosing to be with the partner and only being able to visit their own world but is a full immersion in the new reality to the exclusion of the old. Stories that discuss a partner returning to visit their own world inevitably end tragically, as we see when Oisín begs Niamh to visit Ireland only to fall from his horse, instantly age 300 years, and die. Fairy spouses that choose or are taken into the human world live fully within it, either becoming human themselves as we see in the story of the kelpie who weds a human girl,[23] or eventually returning to their own world, often heartbroken. Humans who are taken into Fairy and are not quickly rescued from it cannot safely return and must instead live out their existence in that realm or die, as Oisín did, when the time they missed on earth catches up to them upon their return. Nonetheless many accounts of fairy lovers and wives end with the human disappearing into the Otherworld never to be seen again. King Arthur loses his knight, Lanval, in this fashion, after he rides away with his fairy mistress.[24]

There are only a few accounts of what we might call 'long distance marriages' where the human remains living on earth and is regularly visited by the fairy spouse, mostly found in the Arthurianesque material such as Lancelet and Ogier the Dane. It would seem that to choose marriage with a fairy – or to be forced into it – means one partner must make a choice to give up their own world, or be stolen from it.

Rules for Otherworldly Marriage

There are some basic rules that seem to exist across folklore for marriage between fairies and humans, which will be outlined here.

- Persuasion is often required for one partner (Gibson, 1955). One partner usually is advocating for the relationship while the other, human or fairy, is reluctant to engage in it. Even in cases where love seems to be a factor this is often in play, for example, Connla takes a month to decide to go with his fairy woman and in Ogier the Dane[25] Ogier goes through multiple trials and two human wives before accepting the fairy woman's love. Obviously in forced marriages this persuasion is even more extreme.

- The human partner is usually put under some form of prohibition in order to equalize the partnership (Spyra, 2020). Spyra suggests that there is an inherent power imbalance in these relationships which is addressed through the use of prohibitions which help to empower the human so long as they are adhered to. Certainly, it is common in these stories to see the human partner explicitly given a thing they must do or must not do to retain their fairy spouse – for example, Pressyne told her mortal husband he couldn't see her birth her children nor bath them and left when he violated that, and similarly her daughter Melusine prohibited her human husband from seeing her on Saturdays and left him when he did so. In the story of Macha the Fairy Woman, Macha prohibits her human husband from telling anyone of her presence, and the eponymous Sir Lanval is put under the same prohibition by his fairy lover. Byrne argues that taboos in these cases *"not only construct a space apart from conventional morality, but they can also enable a further stage of ethical development"*. (Byrne, 2016). The human is shifted away from normal human mores and towards the sometimes inscrutable ethics of Fairy, so that they occupy a liminal space between the two, and are challenged to maintain that liminality by maintaining the taboo.

In the case of forced marriages this taboo is demonstrated differently, through a secret the human must keep whether that is the location of the selkie's sealskin or the knothole the mare entered through. If the fairy finds the source of the magic that's binding them to the human they will flee.

Broken promises or prohibitions result in immediate dissolution of the marriage. Across all the stories this rule seems to exist without exception. To betray a fairy spouse is to lose that fairy spouse, and often lose anything you have gained since they came to you. Fairy wives will return to the place they came from, taking with them their own possessions and often any children who have been produced. Selkie wives who find their hidden sealskin leave immediately, even those that seem to have formed a genuine affection for their mortal spouse, and may or may not take their children with them. Humans taken into fairy voluntarily who break a promise or prohibition are immediately expelled, often leaving them insane or pining away for their lost spouse.

- That which belongs to the fairy spouse remains with the fairy spouse (Gibson, 1955). Although we might imagine fairy marriages as somewhat equal within themselves folklore paints a different picture, often implying that even when the fairy is in the human world, they retain greater control, able to bring luck or financial success or withhold it and retaining possession of everything they brought with them or add to the marriage (as discussed above).

- Children are possible but must choose one world to live in. A common theme across these stories is that fairy-human marriages do result in children but that these children must choose a single world to live in, despite their mixed heritage. In some cases, the child ultimately goes to the Otherworld with their fairy parent while in others they remain in the human world with their human parent; if staying in the human world they are often notably odd or unusual and have a reputation for uncanniness (Gundarsson, 2007).

This summarizes the details within the concept of fairy human marriages, across a range of Western European beliefs. I would suggest that just as the borrowed midwife and stolen bride are common motifs within folklore the fairy marriage occupies a similar space and is deserving of similar consideration. It is, at the least, something found across 1500 years of folklore and across all of Western European material dealing with Otherworldly beings.

III. Modern Accounts

The modern concept of fairies has diversified from the older views, expanding to encompass a range of spirits that include the older folkloric views as well as Victorian and new age ideas, popcultural concepts, and personal gnosis[26] independent from other sources. The definition of marriage applied to all proceeding material is continued here. This section accepts any being labelled as a fairy by a source as such without attempting to analyse the source's criteria in using the term. This section also relays anecdotal and memorate material at face value without any judgement on the source's veracity and views all modern accounts of fairy interactions as 21st century folklore in process. Reviewing these modern accounts is vital in establishing the ongoing nature of this belief and examining how it relates to older beliefs.

There are abundant examples of fairy and human marriages across folklore and literature, however, the phenomena can also be found in 19th century esoteric communities, notably the Golden Dawn, as well as modern 20th and 21st century anecdotes and memorates, particularly among the neopagan and witchcraft communities. These accounts form a clear pattern of modern belief and practice which while focused broadly within certain spiritual communities isn't limited to one specific religion or narrow belief system: those surveyed here encompass a range from various forms of witchcraft to Norse heathenry to eclectic spirituality.

In the mid 1880's SL MacGregor Mathers, leader of the Hermetic Order of the Golden Dawn, an occult society, produced a work entitled *Elemental Theory* which in part suggested that sexual congress was possible between humans and elemental spirits (Nagle, 2007). This concept was drawn from the writings on elementals by the 16th century alchemist Paracelsus, which discusses the various offspring those beings produce with various other beings, and the 1670 novel "Le Comte de Gabalis" which is a satire but which does discuss marriage between humans and spirits, as well as various subsequent other novels and stories, including Melusine and Ondine. Mathers created a marriage ritual for humans and elementals, suggesting it to at least one female Golden Dawn member (Nagel, 2007). While the actual ritual has been lost, along with *Elemental Theory*, and is only know of from references in various letters, its existence and the discourse around it may have had an impact on the later 20th and 21st century practices, and certainly stands as evidence of the endurance of the concept of human marriages to spirits. Theosophy founder Helena Blavatsky also discusses marriages between humans and elementals, which she argued were both possible and potentially dangerous (Nagel, 2007). Blavatsky's writing on the subject must also be considered as a possible influence, particularly given the profound impact Theosophy has had on the understanding of fairies among neopagans.

The idea of human marriage to fairies has lingered on the fringes of folk belief, and in modern witchcraft communities may be influenced by both MacGregor Mathers work and the previous texts which inspired him. The wider patterns noted in the above sections around fairy and human relationships can also be seen in the modern accounts although most of the people contributing them[27] mention having no prior or no significant prior knowledge of fairy folklore or understanding of any historic precedent for fairy and human marriages.

As with the older accounts many modern people who describe being in such a marriage say that they did not seek out either the relationship or the fairy contact. In a personal correspondence to the author, Bat Collazo describes meeting a fairy man and developing a relationship with him via artistic expressions, ritual, and divination which eventually grew into what Collazo described as a courtship culminating in marriage. An anonymous modern witch recorded in Lee Morgan's book *A Deed Without a Name* describes a "spirit man" who she perceived throughout her life but with whom she began a sexual relationship in her 20s and another in the same source described knowing his "fetch-mate"[28] for a period of time before he understood who or what the being was (Morgan, 2012). In contrast Blythe Rhymer, author of the blog 'The Raven and the Lotus' says that while her sidhe husband only came to her in 2019 the two had a past life connection and were married previously and perpetually (Rhymer, 2020). In a middle ground of sort between these two approaches we find author Rionagh na Ard who described a sidhe man who began to work with her in a spiritual context and was eventually revealed as her sidhe soulmate through a connection which existed in a prior incarnation; once this realization happened Rionagh came to realize this same spirit had always been with her throughout her life (Rionagh na Ard, 2014). Rhymer also notes that after becoming aware of the presence of her sidhe husband she came to see that he had been with her throughout her life, echoing sentiments expressed across sources that while the realization of the fairy's presence might come at a specific point, the person would feel or realize that the beings had always been with them in some sense (Morgan, 2012; Rionagh na Ard, 2014; Rhymer, 2020).

The examples we have across past folklore are heteronormative, however, the 21st century expressions are not; this may be because of changing social mores, the demographic today which is most likely to engage with and share these accounts, or the largely heteronormative bias across older accounts. Lee Morgan shares the words of a male witch who has a male fetch-mate, in alignment with the witch's own sexual preference, and Cozallo describes zir spirit husband as "queer"; author Orion Foxwood, who practices a spirituality he calls Faery Seership, describes his fairy spouse as female despite his human world partner being male (Rose, 2020).

It should also be noted that multiple accounts including those from Rhymer, Cozallo, Foxwood, and Rose[29] describe their fairies as either explicitly polyamorous or accepting of the human partner also having human lovers or spouses. This echoes some of the older folkloric accounts, such as the Orkney tale of the man who had both a human wife and fairy wife (Towrie, 2022). There are also accounts of modern fairy relationships that are monogamous between fairy and human, in some cases beginning when the human was in another relationship which was disrupted in favour of the fairy partner (Rose, 2020; anonymous personal correspondence, 2023).

One distinct difference between older folklore accounts and modern anecdotes and memorates is that modern accounts rarely include the taboos that were a hallmark of older stories. The fairy lovers and spouses of today don't often require their human partner to adhere to a firm rule of behaviour under threat of abandonment; rather than Macha or sir Lanval's prohibition against the human partner telling others of his fairy wife modern respondents feel free to share their stories and experiences. In some cases, the person even feels compelled or required to share their story with others (Rhymer, personal correspondence, 2023). Orion Foxwood discusses how his fairy wife is the source of some of his teaching material and that he views his work and writing with and through her as their child, co-created and meant to last beyond him (Rose, 2020). This iteration of fairy marriage belief then exists with a strong public face in contrast to the older belief that such unions required discretion.

Another notable change from older accounts is the lack of physicality of the fairy partner. While older accounts always presuppose the fairy is physically present and interacting with the human in the waking world[30] 21st century accounts generally speak of the fairy partner as being encountered in dreams, visions, or trance states. In instances where a source describes the fairy being present when they are awake the fairy is not visible to ordinary vision, not seen by others,[31] and not physically perceived as a human would be. Some of the anonymous sources in Morgan's book describe the feeling of being touched in waking reality but say it is different than normal touch, lighter or colder, for example (Morgan, 2012).

In general, across the surveyed sources, the purpose of the marriage often aligns with previous or current spiritual work on the human's part, so that the fairy becomes a romantic partner but also a type of spiritual guide as well. This is, of course, in contrast to the older folklore where the union was often either somewhat inexplicable or else seemed to be engaged in for procreative purposes. As with older accounts, however, modern accounts include discussion of the fairy partner supporting the human partner with both healing and financial luck and some mention the human partner's belief they will one day join, or rejoin, the fairy partner in the Otherworld (Rionagh na Ard, 2014; Rose, 2020). The marriage in this context is viewed as existing beyond the human lifetime and reflecting a deeper tie between the fairy and human.

I should note that one person, who wished to remain anonymous, did share that they had a fairy spouse but were prohibited from publicly speaking about them or claiming them, in line with older taboos. Several personal correspondents, who also preferred to remain anonymous, given the nature of the topic, said that they believed their child was the result of a union with their fairy spouse, often through the medium of the fairy possessing their human partner during conception.

Evidence of fairy and human romances and marriages extend back to the oldest written accounts around these beliefs and forward to today. Just as fairies seem to be an intrinsic part of folklore so too is the idea of intimate relationships between fairies and humans which extends beyond the sexual. The exact nature of the accounts varies across older folklore and literature, and modern accounts, while clearly rooted in the same wider beliefs, reflect changing societal mores as well as changing understandings of who and what fairies are, nonetheless wider patterns can be perceived throughout the corpus of material. Despite this fluidity in belief and evolving perception the core ideas have remained across the centuries reflecting the idea that fairies and humans may sometimes marry each other, a true blending of the two worlds. It remains to be seen what direction the beliefs will go in as we progress further into the 21st century and how the ideas around fairy and human marriage will adapt to the ever-changing world, but it seems safe to say that the beliefs will continue to persist in one form or another.

Chapter 10

Frequently Asked Questions

While we have covered a great deal of ground thus far in the various aspects of both beliefs around fairies and sex and the intersection of humans and fairies, there are some niche aspects of the subjects that we haven't gotten to but which I am nonetheless often asked about. As the inspiration for this book was a question that hadn't yet been publicly answered I thought it apt to conclude with an array of other questions I am often asked about or that are related to this subject. These are questions which reflect the sexual mores of the 21st century and aspects of interactions with these beings that – as far as I know – do not generally appear across older written material. They are also questions which may or may not have definitive answers based on the range of folklore but which often at least lean into older material, so that some conclusions may be drawn.

Proceed with the understanding that this chapter in particular will have, basically, all the content warnings one might imagine applying around the subject of sex.

Oral sex – this one was inspired by a Tumblr post that went viral for a time, effectively arguing over whether oral sex with fairies could be considered on par with eating fairy food, and if it would have similar consequences. It is surprisingly difficult to answer from a purely folkloric perspective: on one hand we do have a great deal of evidence that the reason one shouldn't eat or drink things in the world of Fairy is that it is the act of taking these things into one's body that bind the person to that world; in contrast we also have a lot of evidence that a key point is whether food or drink is part of an equal trade or is offered without the human giving in return. By the first logic than yes, oral sex given to a fairy would act to bind the human to that world. However, by the logic of the second theory the human and fairy would be in an equal exchange situation where the human wouldn't be bound by the activity. Unsurprisingly this isn't a subject that directly comes up in the older material, at least to my knowledge, but I personally think I'd lean towards the second possibility being more likely.

Condoms & birth control & abortion – As far as I have been able to ascertain across the folklore and modern accounts, Tolkien had the right of this one; Otherworldly beings seem only to conceive or father a child by their own choice or intentionally. While we have many accounts of humans who unintentionally end up with a baby by or with their fairy lover the opposite doesn't seem to be true, and in many stories the fairy partner seems to be aware that the baby will be or has been conceived. There aren't any older accounts involving birth control of any sort, and as far as I'm aware the only reference to abortion with a fairy lover would be in the ballad of Tam Lin where the female protagonist in some versions goes back to the fairy wood to look for an abortifacient herb, only to be dissuaded from following through by her fairy lover.

Circumcision – this would not be a thing for the vast majority of fairy beings, with a small exception perhaps for those who were part of a religion that practiced circumcision or who had been such as a human in their former lives, if they were stolen humans originally.

Is there a fairy version of tindr/grindr? – you might be surprised how often I am asked some version of this, or you might not be surprised at all. The answer is no, although it will be interesting to see where this goes as folklore about fairies adapts to modern technology. There is at least one spell found in a grimoire that was aimed at gaining the magician a fairy lover, but it is overtly coercive in nature.

Fairies and STIs? – there are no references to any sort of fairy sexually transmitted infections in the older folklore or modern accounts. One might perhaps argue that there may be a magical compulsion that comes with romantic interactions with some types of fairies and metaphorically infects the human and can cause them to become ill or pine away, but that would not be a literal disease or physical condition.

Can fairies be asexual? – in the older material and much of the current accounts, they do not appear to be and in contrast we have a large amount of explicitly sexual material connected to these beings. But since the Victorian era there has been an increase in depictions of asexual fairies that has grown hand in hand with the infantilization of fairies. In modern belief you will find fairies depicted this way, most often in more new age approaches but not exclusively.

Can fairies be arosexual? – Fairies appear across folklore as both romantically and sexually interested in humans, but the two do not always coincide. There are accounts where fairies appear to be arosexual, that is interested in sexual encounters with humans but not in romantic ones; these most often appear in what we might classify as 'one night stand' fairy stories where a human has a single sexual encounter with a fairy being that isn't repeated and doesn't encounter or experience that being again afterwards.

Are fairies androgynous? – yes, they can be, although it varies across the folklore. The Norse alfar are probably the best example of androgyny in older material, with male elves often being described as extremely beautiful and terms for elves being applied to human women to indicate great beauty. That said the idea that all fairies are or must be androgynous is inaccurate, because we do have many stories of overtly gendered fairies.

Conclusion

"Harp and carp, Thomas," she said,
"Harp and carp along wi' me,
And if ye dare to kiss my lips,
Sure of your bodie I will be."
"Betide me weal, betide me woe,
That weird shall never daunton me;"
Syne he has kissed her rosy lips,
All underneath the Eildon Tree.
"Now, ye maun go wi me," she said,
"True Thomas, ye maun go wi me,
And ye maun serve me seven years,
Thro weal or woe, as may chance to be."
Ballad of Thomas the Rhymer

Fairies across the breadth of Celtic and British folklore,
literature, and anecdotal accounts have embodied the outcast,
the forbidden, the threshold, and those things that are socially
disallowed. Anglo-Saxon accounts describe beings that are
male, effeminate and androgynous, but deeply sexual in nature
and action, or female beings with strong martial activities. The
fairies of Medieval literature, usually female, are alluring and
inherently sexual, seducing male protagonists and offering
treasures and power in exchange for sexual favours. In the
Scottish ballad material we find Fairy Queens who hunt, ride,
and rule as men would be expected to; in anecdotal accounts
from the Scottish witch trials fairies appear as sexual partners
to humans while also both teaching them and sometimes
threatening them or physically harming them. In the Victorian
era and into the modern day, fairies came to be depicted across
fiction and artwork as childlike and androgynous. During times
of turbulence and repression fairies represented excess, joy, and

passion even in their malevolence, and in times of greater moral freedom and acceptance of sexuality and gender expressions fairies, for some, have come to represent asexuality and innocence. The one constant as fairies have evolved in relation to humans through the centuries is their place as transgressors of human rules and social expectations. They appear both within and outside the human concept of gender and sexuality, sometimes simultaneously, and they appear to use the human system to their own advantage for reproduction and to prey on humanity. Unlike the humans of the various time periods and places the fairies are found in, these beings move between what humans accept and what they reject for gender roles as it pleases them. In turn, humans who take on the mantle or title of fairy use this pattern to assume that same fluidity and to act in ways that may defy or reject what their society expects of them. Fairies reflect the human world and upend it, as do the humans who mimic them to find acceptance of behaviour otherwise judged unacceptable.

Sex and love with fairies is a risky business. There are a variety of fairies who are seen as implicitly sexual and deadly by nature such as the Leannán sidhe, and Gean Cánach, discussed in Chapter 3, both of whom in modern popular belief seduce the unwary and drain their life force. Keats epic poem 'La Belle Dame sans Merci' depicts a fairy woman who seduces mortal men and leaves them to slowly waste away and there are also a multitude of fairy encounters in anecdotal accounts which feature heavy sexual themes and potential physical consequences for the human, sometimes including death or violations of consent. In the Scottish witchcraft trial accounts, which relayed anecdotal experiences connected to fairies, accused witch, Andro Man, claimed the Fairy Queen offered to do him good and teach him healing skills but only after killing one of his cows; Elspeth Reoch was given the ability to see fairies but was coerced into having sex with a fairy man and Isobell Strathaquin similarly had to have sex with a fairy man in order to gain her magical abilities (Henderson & Cowan: 84). Yet across the breadth of the material we also find stories of fairy sex and love that have a happy ending: Thomas of Erceldoune's Fairy Queen returns him to earth but folklore tells us that she called him back to her later and kept him with her; Niamh and Oisín's story ends tragically but Connla lives happily with his fairy woman as does Nera; Andro Man had a relationship with the Fairy Queen which spanned 30 years.

There are few constants with fairies, except perhaps that they persist no matter how many generations across centuries have declared them gone or a relic of past generations. They evolve as human cultures evolve and they remain fixed to human belief, a reflection of the sexual mores of each group and an inversion of gendered roles. Fairies are all the things that humans wish they could be, and fear, and are denied. They are indulgent where humans must be thrifty, they are joyous where expressions of joy are restricted, they are overtly sexual when sex is to be denied and they are equally asexual when sex is culturally embraced. They are, in short, a mirror held up to human cultures which reflects but inverts what it sees.

The question that inspired this text, and the articles which it was expanded from, asked about sex and gender among fairies, whether they were heteronormative or not. The answer is 'all of the above'. Fairies, elves, diverse Otherworldly beings, are gendered and not, are sexual and not, are every possibility the human imagination can conjure. They can be androgynous and asexual, they can move between forms, they can be innocent or debauched, but the one through line to all the stories across the last millennia and across much of western Europe is that they are tied to humanity through both love and sex.

Thomas the Rhymer is brought into the Fairy Queen's service with a kiss, and Elph Erving is similarly paid with a kiss. A simple kiss binds each to Fairy and irreversibly changes their lives in each story, for good and for ill, irrevocably moving them away from humanity and breaking the social expectations around them. And perhaps ultimately that's the answer to the question of sex and gender among fairies – its dangerously transgressive and transformative.

Bibliography

Acland, A., (1997) Thomas Off Erceldoune; Thomas the Rhymer Appendix Retrieved from http://www.tam-lin.org/library/thomas_text.html

Ashliman, D., (2005) Night-Mares http://www.pitt.edu/~dash/nightmare.html

Bassin, E., (1977) *Old Songs of Skye*

Black, G., (1903). *County Folk-Lore*, vol. 3: Examples of Printed Folk-Lore Concerning the Orkney & Shetland Islands

Blavatsky, H., (1893) Elementals Retrieved from https://www.theosophy.world/resource/elementals-hp-blavatsky

Botelho, L., (2015) 'Old Women and Sex: Fear, Fantasy, and a Defining Life Course in Early-Modern Europe', *Clio, Women, Gender, History*, no 42

Briggs, K., (1967) *The Fairies in Tradition and Literature*

Buccola, R., (2006) *Fairies, Fractious Women, and the Old Faith: Fairy Lore in Early Modern British Drama and Culture*

Burson, A., (1983) 'Swan Maidens and Smiths: A study of "Völundarkviða"', *Scandinavian Studies*, vol 55, no 1

Carbery, Ethna., (1902). 'The Love Talker', The Four Winds of Eirinn. Retrieved from https://digital.library.upenn.edu/women/carbery/eirinn/eirinn.html#talker

Child, F., (1882) *The English and Scottish Popular Ballads* vol 1 – 5

Cooper, H., (2006) Lancelot's Wives, Arthuriana vol 16 no 2 Retrieved from https://www.jstor.org/stable/27870759

Douglas, G., (1900) *Scottish Folk and Fairy Tales*

The Dublin and London magazine. (1826). Retrieved from https://www.google.com/books/edition/_/cn4EAAAAQAAJ?hl=en&gbpv=1&bsq=ganconer

Dúchas (2022) A Fairy Wedding The Schools' Collection, Volume 1003, Page 391 Retrieved from https://www.duchas.ie/en/cbes/5070798/5065014/5100207

— (2024) Gean-canach The Schools' Collection, Volume 0983, Page 370. Retrieved from https://www.duchas.ie/en/cbes/5170141/5169210

Dunnigan, S., (2016) 'From Fairy Queens to Ogresses: Female Enchanters in Early Scottish Literature', *The Bottle Imp*, Issue 20

Fisher, W., (2001) 'The Renaissance Beard: Masculinity in Early Modern England', *Renaissance Quarterly*, vol 54, no 1

Gibson, H., (1955) The Human-Fairy Marriage Retrieved https://www.tandfonline.com/doi/abs/10.1080/0015587X.1955.9717488?journalCode=rfol20

Gilfillan, G., (1855) The Poetical Works of John Dryden. Retrieved from https://chaucer.fas.harvard.edu/wife-bath-her-tale

The Great Selkie of Sule Skerrie, Mainly Norfolk; https://mainlynorfolk.info/steeleye.span/songs/greatsilkieofsuleskerry.html

Green, R., (2016) *Elf Queens and Holy Friars: Fairy Beliefs and the Medieval Church*

Grimm, J., (1888) *Teutonic Mythology*

Gundarsson, K., (2007) *Elves, Wights, and Trolls*

Haas, Natascha., (2004). "A fundamentally religious and Catholic work" – Who is the saviour in J.R.R. Tolkien's The Lord of the Rings?

Hall, A., (2007) *Elves in Anglo-Saxon England*, The Boydell Press, 2007

Hallgrimsdottir, H., (2005) Elf Truths Blogspot Retrieved from http://elftruths.blogspot.com/

Harms, D., Clark, J., and Peterson, J., (2015) *The Book of Oberon*

Heddle, D., (2016) 'Selkies, Sex, and the Supernatural', *The Bottle Imp*, issue 20

Henderson, L., and C., (2008) Edward, *Scottish Fairy Belief*

Hughes, B., (2014) *Demon Lovers: Embracing the Monster in Paranormal Romance*

Huisman, R., (2008) 'Narrative Sociotemporality and Complementary Gender Roles in Anglo-Saxon Society: the relevance of wifmann and woepnedmann to a plot summary of the old English poem Beowulf', Journal of the Australian Early Medieval Association

Hunt, R., (1903) *Popular Romances of the West of England*

Jewell, W., (1611) The Golden Cabinet of True Treasure; Early English Books Online Text Creation Partnership, 2011, Retrieved from http://name.umdl.umich.edu/A04486.0001.001

Jones, M., (2022) The Physicians of Myddfai Retrieved from https://www.maryjones.us/ctexts/myddfai.html

Karras, R., (2005) *Sexuality in Medieval Europe: Doing Unto Others*

Keating, G., (1902) *Foras Feasa ar Eirinn*

Keats, J., (1988) 'La Belle Dame sans Merci', Penguin Classics Selected Poems

Kennedy-Fraser, M., and MacCloud, K., (1909) *Songs of the Hebrides*

Kirk, R., and Lang, A., (1893) The Secret Commonwealth of Elves, Fauns, and Fairies

Laskaya, A., and Salisbury, E., (1995) The Middle English Breton Lays. Retrieved from https://d.lib.rochester.edu/teams/text/laskaya-and-salisbury-middle-english-breton-lays-sir-launfal

Lawerence, J., (2009) 'Tam Lin's Garden', *Goblin Fruit*, Autumn 2009

Lennard, J., (2010) Of Sex and Faerie: further essays on genre fiction

Lidman, S., (2013) 'Violence or Justice? Gender-specific Structures and Strategies in Early Modern Europe', *The History of the Family*, vol 18 issue 3

Mackenzie, D., (1935) *Scottish Folk-lore and Folk Life*

Magliocco, S., (2018) '"Reconnecting to Everything": Fairies in Contemporary Paganism' in Fairies, Demons, and Nature Spirits: 'Small Gods' at the Margins of Christendom

— (2019) 'The Taming of the Fae: Literary and Folkloric Fairies in Modern Paganism' in Magic and Witchery in the Modern West: Celebrating the Twentieth Anniversary of 'Triumph of the Moon'

McNeil, H., (2001), The Celtic Breeze: Stories of the Otherworld from Scotland, Ireland, and Wales

Morag and the Kelpie https://terreceltiche.altervista.org/morag-and-the-kelpie/

Morgan, L., (2012) A Deed Without a Name

Nagel, A., (2007). Marriage with Elementals: From "Le Comte de Gabalis" to a Golden Dawn ritual. Retrieved from https://www.academia.edu/4046657/Marriage_with_Elementals_From_Le_Comte_de_Gabalis_to_a_Golden_Dawn_ritual

Narvaez, P., (1991) 'Newfoundland Berry Pickers "In The Fairies"', The Good People

Narvaez, P., (1991) 'Social functions of Fairylore', The Good People

Ó Crualaoich, G., (2003) The Book of the Cailleach

O'Donovan, J., (1856) Annals of the Kingdom of Ireland

Ogier the Dane (2022) William Morris Archive 'Introduction to Ogier the Dane' Retrieved from http://morrisarchive.lib.uiowa.edu/introduction-ogierthedane

Ossianic Society (1854) Transactions of the Ossianic Society

Purkiss, D., (2000) At the Bottom of the Garden

Rhymer, B., (2020) The Raven and the Lotus: That's What Sidhe Said. Retrieved from http://theravenandthelotus.com/a-human-incarnated-sidhe

Rhys, J., (1901) Celtic Folklore: Welsh and Manx

Rionagh na Ard (2014) Awakening: Life Lessons from the Sidhe

Rose, M., (2022) *Spirit Marriage: Intimate Relationships with Otherworldly Beings*

Rosetti, C., (1862) *The Goblin Market and Other Poems*

RWA (2024) About the Romance Genre, Romance Writers of America. Retrieved from https://www.rwa.org/Online/Romance_Genre/About_Romance_Genre.aspx

Sari, M., (2017) 'Fantastic Metamorphoses and the Subversion of Traditional Gender roles in Christina Rossetti's Speaking Likenesses', *Ankara University the Journal of the Faculty of Languages and History-Geography*, 57-2

Silver, C., (1999) *Strange and Secret People: Fairies and Victorian Consciousness*

Spyra, P (2020) *The Liminality of Fairies: Readings in Late Medieval English and Scottish Romance*

Suggs, R., (2018) *Fairies: A Dangerous History*

Theosophy World (2023) Fairies Retrieved from https://www.theosophy.world/encyclopedia/fairies

Thomas Off Erceldoune (1997) Thomas the Rhymer Appendix Retrieved from http://www.tam-lin.org/library/thomas_text.html

Timbers, F., (2016) The Magical Adventures of Mary Parrish: The Occult World of 17th-Century London

Towrie, S., (2022) Mansie O'Kierfa and His Fairy Bride Retrieved from http://www.orkneyjar.com/folklore/fairicks/kierfea.htm

Tyellas (2003) Warm Beds Are Good: Sex and Libido in Tolkien's Writing. Retrieved from https://ansereg.com/WarmBedsareGood.pdf

— (2009) What Tolkien Officially Said About Elf Sex Retrieved from https://ansereg.com/what_tolkien_officially_said_abo.htm?fbclid=IwAR0puERelFslNBx62B6y6n1s5j1aSOAyxp-T-l1rSnCm96d6RI6httiKcK8

Vaccaro, C., and Kisor, Y, eds., (2017) *Tolkien and Alterity*

Wade, J., (2011) *Fairies in Medieval Romance*

Walsh, B., (2002) *The Secret Commonwealth and the Fairy Belief Complex*

Wilby, E., (2005) *Cunningfolk and Familiar Spirits*

Wilde, E., (1887) *Ancient Legends, Mystic Charms, and Superstitions of Ireland*

Williams, N., (1991) 'The Semantics of the Word Fairy: Making Meaning Out of Thin Air', *The Good People*

Wimberly, L., (1965) *Folklore in the English & Scottish Ballads*

Wood, J., (1992) The Fairy Bride Legend in Wales Retrieved from https://www.jstor.org/stable/1261034

Yeats, W. B., (1888) Fairy and Folk Tales of the Irish Peasantry

— (1962) *The Celtic Twilight*

Young, S., (2017) *The Fairy Census*, online pdf

Endnotes

1. Incubus, plural incubi, are a specific type of male demon who is sexual in nature, seducing women and impregnating them. Succubus, plural succubi, are the female version of this demon who come to sleeping men, have intercourse with them, and take their semen.

2. In the older French, fae, by various spellings, was originally a noun indicating a supernatural woman or enchantress and which Williams (463) supposes may then have been used in the form of faerie to indicate the place and taken into English with that meaning. Williams article on the semantics of fairy offers insight into this transition.

3. This obviously involves a lack of consent on the part of the fairy, and should be understood in that context.

4. A notable exception to the wider sexual risk represented by the fairy folk can be found in the lore of selkies. Although sex often plays a role in the folklore around these beings, commonly resulting in children, the dynamic is different and rarely dangerous. Female selkies are usually unwilling partners in these stories, captured by fisherman who find and take the selkie's magical seal skin trapping her until she can recover it. Male selkies may be casual trysts or more involved lovers but do not seem to present inherent risk to a human partner. Heddle discusses this in more depth in her article 'Selkies, Sex, and the Supernatural'.

5. We will be leaving out the shoemaking elves and Santa's elves, who wouldn't have much of a place in this text anyway.

6. I should note that some scholars have suggested that selkie folklore is a misunderstanding of encounters with indigenous, specifically Inuit, people. While this is only a theory on the origins of the beliefs it does cast the selkie-wife stories in a different light.

7. I am following the various dictionaries here in translating sidhe as fairy in this context, but I will note that there is an ongoing controversy about this and some people prefer the term not be translated or be given as something closer to 'Otherworldly' hill or being to avoid the implicit associations the word fairy has in modern English.

8. It is unusual in my experience to find the Irish aos sidhe referred to as incubi although they are often referred to as demons, specifically demons of the air. However, referring to the Leannán sidhe as an incubus here makes some sense both because it is being recorded by a Catholic priest and also because the spirit had been sexually oppressive to a young woman.

9. Buachalán – ragweed

10. Translation:

> He found in the pavilion/ the King's daughter of Olyroun/ Dame Tryamour she was called/ her father was the King of Fairy/
>
> of the west both near and far/ a man of great might/ In the pavilion he found a sumptuous bed/ that was covered in linen/
>
> therein lay the gracious lady/ that after Sir Launfal had sent/ that lovely one glittered brightly

11. Translated by me from the original trial transcript, as given by Hall, 2007:

> "...the elphis hes shapes and claythhes lyk men, and that thay will have fair covert taiblis, and that they ar bot schaddowis, bot starker nor men, and that thay have playing and dansing quhen thay pleas; and als that the quene is verray plesand, and wilbe auld and young quhen scho pleissis; scho mack any kyng scho pleisis, and lyis with any scho lykis."
>
> ["the elves have shapes and clothes like men, and they will have fair covered tables, and that they are but

shadows, but stronger than men, and that they have playing and dancing when they please; and also that the queen is very pleasant, and will be old and young when she pleases; she makes any king she pleases and lays with any she likes."]

12. The virginity toll is one of three options, the other two being a gold ring or green mantle.

13. An elemental being in this modern lens is a creature that embodies or exists as the manifested spirit of one of the four classical elements: earth, air, fire, or water.

14. See the collected material in Simon Young's 'Fairy Census 2014 – 2017' for multiple examples of these types of encounters, such as 4, 6, 9, 19, 23, 24.

15. Examples include the movies Tinkerbell, Epic, Strange Magic, and Fern Gully.

16. Slash fic is a concept found in fan fiction where two (or more) characters are paired together romantically or sexually who did not have that relationship in canon. Beginning with Star Trek fan fiction in the 1970's slash fic has grown to be extremely popular subgenre which allows fan fic authors to explore diverse subjects and to give characters the stories the fan feels they had or should have had, often based on subtext within the canon.

17. In this it differs not at all from human marriage.

18. Lancelot's species is ambiguous, in some versions he is the son of the Lady of the Lake, a fairy woman, while in others he is a human raised by fairies. I am including him here in the category of fairies despite this ambiguity.

19. In fairness Finn may not have actually been human but he is presented as such in most of the stories.

20. As discussed at a few points already Selkies are generally not referred to as fairies, per se, but are more generally Otherworldly beings found across folklore often adjacent

to fairy beliefs. I am including them here under this wider concept.

21. The story of Goodwin Wharton and Mary Parrish is complex and convoluted, with Wharton – a member of parliament – often being assumed insane and Parrish thought of as a grifter taking advantage of his mental illness. Nonetheless it is also much tied up with fairies, although tangential to this current book. Parrish convinced Wharton to marry a Fairy Queen and afterwards that he was himself a king of the Fairy world.

22. Briggs discusses this at length in a chapter in *Fairies in Tradition and Literature*.

23. See McNeill, pp 68-72.

24. I'd note this also offers a very interesting reversal of the usual story of the maiden riding off behind her knight after being rescued; here it is Lanval who is rescued by the fairy woman and who is brought up behind her on her horse to be carried off to safety.

25. Long distance or intermittent relationships are more common in folklore of fairy lovers, rather than spouses per se.

26. Personal gnosis is defined as knowledge that an individual gains through a spiritual experience which may or may not be supported by outside sources.

27. Notable exceptions being the authors like Rionagh na Ard and Blythe Rymer who were explicitly engaging with folkloric fairy related material or beliefs before their own encounters began.

28. Fetch mate is the term used in some forms of Traditional Witchcraft to denote a fairy being or spirit who is permanently attached to a human. Sometimes also called a fetch bride. The terms fetch and fairy are used interchangeably in Morgan's book.

29. Rose is the author of *Spirit Marriage* a book which includes a survey of various modern people who describe themselves having fairy or spirit spouses, however, she also includes her own personal accounts of her fairy husband in the book as well.

30. Gearóid Ó Crualaoich in his *Book of the Cailleach* describes a late 19th century Irish wise woman who had a fairy lover who was seen with her by multiple witnesses, showing that this older folklore of physical fairies did extend until relatively recently.

31. Although it should be noted that multiple people described others perceiving their fairy spouse's presence, usually via extra sensory perception, clairvoyance, or similar means.

About the Author

Morgan Daimler is a witch who has been a polytheist since the early '90's. Following a path inspired by the Irish Fairy Faith blended with neopagan witchcraft. Morgan teaches classes on Irish myth and magical practices, fairies, and related subjects in the United States and internationally. Morgan has been published in multiple anthologies as well as in Witches and Pagans magazine, and Pagan Dawn magazine, and she is one of the world's foremost experts on all things Fairy.

Pagan Portals (Celtic)
Lugh
Brigid
Aos Sidhe
The Dagda
The Morrigan
Irish Paganism
Raven Goddess
Manannán mac Lir
Gods and Goddesses of Ireland

Pagan Portals (Fairy)
Living Fairy
Fairy Queens
Fairy Witchcraft
21st Century Fairy

Pagan Portals (Norse)
Odin
Thor
Freya

Other Moon Books
Pantheon – The Norse
Travelling the Fairy Path
A New Dictionary of Fairies
Fairies A Guide to the Celtic Fair Folk
Fairy – The Otherworld by Many Names
Fairycraft – Following the Path of Fairy Witchcraft
Where the Hawthorn Grows – An American Druid's reflections

Readers of ebooks can buy or view any of these bestsellers by clicking on the live link in the title. Most titles are published in paperback and as an ebook. Paperbacks are available in traditional bookshops. Both print and ebook formats are available online.

Find more titles and sign up to our readers' newsletter www.collectiveinkbooks.com/paganism

For video content, author interviews and more, please subscribe to our YouTube channel.

MoonBooksPublishing

Follow us on social media for book news, promotions and more:

Facebook: Moon Books

Instagram: @MoonBooksCI

X: @MoonBooksCI

TikTok: @MoonBooksCI